First Light

Mark Hayhurst's television dramas include *37 Days*, *The Man Who Crossed Hitler*, *London's Burning* and *Animals*. His documentaries include *To Stop a Tyrant*, *The Promised Land*, *Terror – Robespierre and the French Revolution*, *The Last Days of the Raj*, *The Year London Blew Up*, *The Somme*, *American Dream*, *Challenger – Go for Launch*, *Brinks-Mat – the Greatest Heist*, *Days in the Life*, *Witchcraze* and *The Difficult Birth of the NHS*. For the stage, he has also written *Taken At Midnight*.

First Light

Mark Hayhurst

First Light

Bloomsbury Methuen Drama
An imprint of Bloomsbury Publishing Plc

BLOOMSBURY
LONDON · OXFORD · NEW YORK · NEW DELHI · SYDNEY

Bloomsbury Methuen Drama

An imprint of Bloomsbury Publishing Plc

Imprint previously known as Methuen Drama

50 Bedford Square	1385 Broadway
London	New York
WC1B 3DP	NY 10018
UK	USA

www.bloomsbury.com

**BLOOMSBURY, METHUEN DRAMA and the Diana logo
are trademarks of Bloomsbury Publishing Plc**

First published 2016

© Mark Hayhurst 2016

British Library Cataloguing-in-Publication Data
A catalogue record for this book is available from the British Library.

ISBN: PB: 978-1-3500-1246-2
ePDF: 978-1-3500-1243-1
ePub: 978-1-3500-1244-8

Library of Congress Cataloging-in-Publication Data
A catalog record for this book is available from the Library of Congress

Cover design by Olivia D'Cruz.
Texture designed by Freepix.
Cover image by SWD for Chichester Festival Theatre Production

Typeset by Mark Heslington Ltd, Scarborough, North Yorkshire
Printed and bound in Great Britain

Preface

Nothing quite prepares you for your first sight of Thiepval, the Memorial to the Missing of the Somme. It's like the first time you see the Grand Canyon or the Taj Mahal. You're already familiar with these places because you've seen them in a thousand pictures and perhaps heard sensational first-hand reports from marvelling friends. But your own actual encounter provokes not the jolt of recognition – often shocking enough in itself – but something close to stupefaction. The Taj Mahal is more scintillating than you thought; the Grand Canyon more monstrous.

I succumbed to this feeling when I first visited Thiepval on the Somme. I had read about the events it commemorated and, before that, been told about them as a young boy. I'd studied the war poets at school and as a teenager had been introduced to Robert Graves's *Goodbye to All That* and Erich Maria Remarque's *All Quiet on the Western Front*. I knew about the vast numbers of war dead, of how they exceeded the populations of famous cities. But once there, in Picardy, gazing for the first time on Sir Edwin Lutyens's gigantic monument, it was impossible not to gasp for air.

Those who've seen it will know what I mean. The construction sits on a gentle brow with a sweep of white tablets commemorating the British and Commonwealth dead on the one side and grey ranks of stone crosses commemorating the French dead on the other. And then, on the monument itself, carved into sheets of white Portland stone, are the names of all the men whose bodies were never found – over 72,000 of them. You can't imagine so many people living in this small rural area, let alone dying there. A catastrophe was enacted in these fields.

And yet, if you can forgive the triteness of the saying, life goes on. The old battlefield is farmland again and around the Lutyens memorial and between the numerous smaller war cemeteries you will see a tractor moving through the fields, a combine harvester turning a half-circle. There's an Auden poem called 'Musée des Beaux Arts' where the poet reflects on how well 'the Great Masters' understood 'suffering' and 'its human position'. An awesome or tragic event is typically accompanied in their paintings, he says, by the continuation of daily life in all its stupid indifference.

Auden notes how the ploughman in Breugel's *Landscape with the Fall of Icarus* turns his back on disaster – in this case the boy falling out of the sky – because he has other things to do. And so it is in present-day Picardy. The catastrophe is permanently on show, but people need to eat and windows need opening.

And yet even now, in the twenty-first century, a soldier's corpse will occasionally appear in the fields of the Somme, disgorged by the movement of the earth below or disturbed by the farmer's plough. No one ignores that. The corpse is re-buried with military honours and if it can somehow be identified, and belongs to one of the 'Missing', that man's name is scrupulously removed from the Portland stone and he shifts his position from one of the 'missing' to one of the 'known'. Less surprisingly, but still alarmingly, shells and cartridges, bits of barbed wire and shrapnel, tin cups, brass buttons and copper money also surface from time to time.

The past is always with us of course, but in these French acres it has settled permanently over the landscape and keeps springing from the earth below. It demands to be acknowledged. It's impossible to forget.

* * *

The idea for this play germinated, I suppose, when I first visited the Somme and Flanders battlefields with a couple of friends in 1994.

We toured the usual sites – the Menin Gate in Ypres, the vast Tyne Cot cemetery cresting Passchendaele, the elegant Canadian memorial at Vimy Ridge that soars like an Apollo launching pad out of the escarpment and the Memorial to the Missing of the Somme. We wandered through some of the smaller cemeteries too, one of them I recall almost entirely full of Sheffield men who had died on the same day. And then in the village of Bailleulmont we saw the headstones, in adjacent plots, belonging to Private Albert Ingham of the 3rd Manchester Pals and his friend Private Alfred Longshaw. Over the years the grave of Albert Ingham, in particular, has become a popular site for pilgrimage. People leave the more beaten paths to work their way to this obscure place. For on Albert Ingham's stone are carved the unique words 'Shot at Dawn'. Both these young men, volunteers from 1914, were executed in 1916, on 1 December, just two of 346 British soldiers of the Great War to lose their lives in this way – a micro tragedy folded inside the macro one. The majority of the 346, like Ingham and Longshaw, had been punished by Field General Court Martial for desertion. But those affecting words, 'Shot at Dawn', only appear on Albert's headstone. For the rest of the 346, at least so far as their memorials are concerned, you would never know.

Such is the accusatory power of the phrase that it's possible to forget that 'Shot at Dawn' is a euphemism. But like many military euphemisms – 'collateral damage', 'concentration camp' – the phrase has acquired a power that the thing it is trying to escape – in this case 'execution by firing squad' – can never hope to match. Dawn is a time of birth and of hope and of potential, a way of scrubbing the record clean and starting again. But all that innocence is subject to mockery when an execution squad assembles at first light.

We talked about those words a long time after our visit, our curiosity stirred not just by the naked declaration 'Shot at Dawn', but also by the remainder of the inscription, which reads 'One of the First to Enlist, a Worthy Son of his Father'. It seemed – and still seems – an amazing report, as well as a deeply loving one. But there was something not quite right about it. Why just the father? Where was the mother in all this? Was the man a widower or did the inscription simply reflect the social conventions of the day? Was there something in the nature of the act of desertion, with its suggestions of cowardice and its proximity to 'shirking', which especially needed a *father's* exculpation? Or had there been a family argument between Albert's parents over whether to put the shocking words on their son's headstone at all? We didn't know, and I still don't know. In fact I didn't want to know when I came to write *First Light*. To better retain the universal element of the story I felt I needed a free hand to speculate.

Since that visit to Bailleulmont in 1994 the debate about First World War executions has moved on considerably. In 2006 something very important happened. After many years lobbying the Labour government issued posthumous pardons to 306 of the executed men (the excluded being the 40 soldiers shot for murder or mutiny). So far as we can tell it was a decision that had the overwhelming weight of public opinion on its side. That weight, in truth, had been growing ever since 1918 when the effort to understand 'shell shock' and what we, today, would call post-traumatic stress disorder and combat stress reaction, began to gather pace. There was something humiliating, it seemed, as well as unjust, about executing men who'd experienced the fulminating industrial horror of this war, especially after military trials that owed more to Roman law than English common law. The more civilians came to understand what the 'Western Front' had meant for the ordinary soldier, the more they were inclined to pity those whose morale had cracked. Certainly Albert Ingham and Alfred Longshaw had seen the worst the Somme could throw up. Both had gone 'over the top' on 1 July, and both had been involved in desperate actions in Montauban and Trones Wood in the first weeks of the battle. Their desertion could never be described as heroic, but perhaps it could be seen as reasonable – the rational outcome of being exposed to too much slaughter, or even the result of imaginations working lucidly and possibly with too much clarity. Certainly between 1939 and 1945 there were no more Albert Inghams and Alfred Longshaws because the British Army had stopped executing men. The lost practice was not lamented.

* * *

One hundred years after their deaths the lives of Albert Ingham and Alfred Longshaw and millions of men like them appear to be still within touching distance. Yet their ordeal – I mean the whole experience of being on the Western Front – seems simultaneously antique. Reading Denis Winter's great book *Death's Men*, you wonder what sort of nation it was that felt it permissible to march men to the front past stacks of freshly cut wooden crucifixes. You read about the incredible rates of attrition and understand that the old concept of 'cannon fodder' actually meant something in 1916. You marvel at the famous stoicism of the British soldier who 'mustn't grumble' and who copes, or appears to cope, with the death all around him by treating it as a joke.

That famous soldiers' song, which encapsulates both the stoicism and the joke – 'We're here because we're here because we're here because we're here' – is something that we can all understand and yet in its resignation it speaks, we hope, of a more deferential age that's now gone. I think it's for this reason that those men who broke the chain of being 'here because we're here', that's to say deserters like Albert Ingham and Alfred Longshaw, appear to strike a more modern, and therefore more accessible, note than those who stayed, forever, in the line of fire.

In *Death's Men* there is a description of how strange and frightening it was for soldiers to leave the security of the trench and go 'over the top' – surely the defining experience of the Great War infantryman. Few men talked about it openly, either at the time or later when looking back. But those who did clearly believed it to be the most intense event of their lives. The whistle went and the climb into no man's land began. Nearly all of them mention being instantly out of breath the moment they emerged above the parapet into the open. Some men underwent what can only be called an out-of-body experience. Others likened the climb to being plunged into an icy bath. In other words, as they left the trench they were gasping for air, pretty much as we gasp for air today, when we see what remains.

Mark Hayhurst

First Light was first produced at Chichester Festival Theatre's Minerva Theatre on 10 June 2016 with the following cast and creative team:

George Ingham	Phil Davis
Agnes Ingham	Kelly Price
Company Sergeant-Major Deakin	Andrew Westfield
Albert (Bert) Ingham	Tom Gill
Alfred (Alfie) Longshaw	David Moorst
Max Henderson	Philip Cumbus
Corporal Quinn	Edward Sayer
Earnshaw	Niall McNamee
Conker	Freddie Watkins
Squire	Alex Jordan
Eliza Ingham	Amelda Brown
Robert	Tom Preston
Tailor	Sam Phillips
Steward	Niall McNamee
Sergeant Emment	Philip Cumbus
Librarian	Edward Sayer
Lieutenant Jennings	Sam Phillips
Parfitt	Alex Jordan
Major-General John Shea	Andrew Woodall

Director	Jonathan Munby
Designer	Paul Wills
Lighting Designer	Tim Mitchell
Composer	Alex Baranowski
Sound Designer	Fergus O'Hare
Casting Director	Gabrielle Dawes
Movement Director	Danny McGrath
Assistant Director	Anthony Lau

First Light

To the memory of Gordon, my dad

Characters

George Ingham
Agnes Ingham
Company Sergeant-Major Deakin
Albert (Bert) Ingham
Alfred (Alfie) Longshaw
Max Henderson
Corporal Quinn
Earnshaw
Conker
Squire
Eliza Ingham
Robert
Tailor
Steward
Sergeant Emment
Librarian
Lieutenant Jennings
Parfitt
Major-General John Shea

Prologue

IMPERIAL WAR GRAVES COMMISSION, LONDON, 1925

The palest of morning lights breaks into a small ante-room where **George Ingham**, *mid-fifties, and his daughter* **Agnes**, *mid-thirties, sit. There's a faint hint of an urban dawn chorus. Both father and daughter are smartly dressed. He's a labourer, she's a school teacher.*

George   I hate the dawn.

Agnes   You used to love it, Dad.

George   For most men it means work of course. Sleep cut short too soon.

Agnes   Which is why it's only you and the poets who've ever seen anything in it.

George   Once perhaps. Not any more.

The birdsong swells a bit. **Albert (Bert) Ingham**, *twenty, in battle dress, walks through the room, oblivious to his surroundings as his surroundings are to him.* **Agnes** *takes hold of* **George**'s *hand.*

Agnes   You will look forward again, Dad. See dawn for what she really is.

The light – first light – comes up on an attack trench on the the Somme, 1 July 1916. **George** *and* **Agnes** *remain on stage throughout.*

Bert *takes his place is the trench next to* **Alfred (Alfie) Longshaw**, *twenty-one. The infernal noise of explosions and flying metal gives way to silence as the guns stop. Other members of the Pals are also at ready, including* **Company Sergeant-Major Deakin**, *a forty-five-year-old Cockney in this Manchester battalion – the 18th Pals' Battalion.*

Deakin   Sixty seconds!

Alfie *is rummaging in the back of his pack*

Bert   You all right?

Alfie *just nods, preoccupied.*

Bert   You sure, Alfie?

Alfie *raises his hand, a bicycle chain wrapped around his fist.*

Bert   Where in hell did you get that from?

Alfie   Brought it wi' me.

Bert   What for?

Alfie (*slipping the pack back on his back*)   Something I saw once, back in Salford.

Bert   What did y . . .

Alfie   And you want to see what Jerry's got. Butchers' knives! That long. No one's playing fair today.

He wraps the bike chain harder, psyching himself up. **Bert** *watches him in amazement and confusion.*

Bert   Keep close to me won't you?

Deakin   Twenty seconds!

Alfie   You'll be right with me, Bert.

Bert   Yeah, but please keep close.

Alfie (*gritted teeth*)   You'll be awreet.

Bert   'Cause it's not far is it?

Alfie   Not far at all.

Deakin   Five seconds.

Alfie (*desperate – psyching himself up*)   A fast bowler's run-up. That's all. And then we'll knock 'em over.

Shouts from the men.

Come on Lancashire!

Shrieking whistle from **Deakin** . . .

*Men start to climb out of the trench. Fade to black. The whistle
continues, machine-gun fire.*

Max Henderson, *a thirty-three year-old civil servant, enters the
ante-room. He wears an outside coat and is taking bicycle clips from
his trouser legs, oblivious at first to* **George** *and* **Agnes** *who rise
out of their seats.*

Max Oh!

Agnes Yes, we're here already.

Max So I see!

Agnes Punctual. Well, more than punctual.

Max Is there such a thing?

Agnes You might know it as 'early'.

Max *laughs.*

Agnes We got the night train from Manchester, so we came
straight here from the station. (*Pause.*) Dad's first time in
London.

Max Ha! Well, it's not Lancashire.

George Few places are.

Max That sounds pretty unassailable. Welcome to the
Commission.

Act One

Scene One

THE SOMME – BEHIND THE LINES, 20 JULY 1916

It's ten miles behind the lines, though there are signs of war damage. A group of Manchester Pals sit on the edge of a crater. Among the group is **Alfie** *who has his head bandaged. Also* **Bert**, **Conker** *(eighteen),* **Earnshaw** *(twenty-eight), and* **Squire** *(twenty-three). They are all fairly spruced up, having slept and washed an hour or so ago.* **Corporal Quinn** *(thirty-five) arrives, with a sackful of 'quick firers', the Field Service Postcards that soldiers liked to send home as soon as they'd left the front line.*

Quinn Quick firers, lads? Come on, boys, don't be shy. Two weeks in the front line . . .

Alfie Three!

Quinn Some one can count. Well done.

Arms now go up.

Three weeks then. And now it's time to tell the folks back home you're in one piece.

He distributes the cards.

Bert You know what I hate about these postcards?

Alfie They're not scented.

Earnshaw Aye, that's an oversight by the army. Not like them to make a mistake like that.

Bert I hate the 'quite'.

Alfie You what?

Bert The 'quite', you know. 'I am *quite* well.'

Alfie You *are* quite well.

Bert No I'm not, I'm very well. We all are. We came through a battle. 'Quite well' sounds like summat's wrong with me. It will do to our mum and dad.

Conker Cross the 'quite' out then.

Quinn If you do that, Conker, it'll never be sent. Tamper with this form in anyway except by erasing the lines where it gives you more than one choice and – it says here, *underlined* – 'the postcard will be destroyed'.

Squire 'Destroyed'! Not just torn up or thrown in't bin but 'destroyed'.

Alfie Well, the Army has to destroy summat out here in France. Good for morale. Jerry's too difficult, so the Field Service Postcard will have to do.

Quinn Well you've been warned. Mess with it and I won't take it back.

He leaves to distribute more further on.

Bert Mum's gonna read it and she'll be worried. (*As his mum.*) 'It says here he's quite well. Why's he only *quite* well?'

Earnshaw See, the thing is, it's officer speak isn't it? When *they* say 'quite' they mean 'very'. (*Posh voice.*) 'I am quite well.' You see?

They look at him like he's mad. But he won't be deterred

'I am *quite* well.' Whole different meaning. Bloody thing's been written for them, not us.

Alfie I'd love one day to cross that middle bit out though. All the stuff about being sick and wounded and being in hospital and just leave the first and last bits. 'I am quite well and . . .

. . . hope to be discharged soon.'

Laughter

Bert   Funny isn't it how 'discharged' means two different things? Gun going off, soldier leaving hospital.

Conker   English language, Bert. It's a wonderful thing. *Nothing means what it says.*

Earnshaw (*looking at* **Alfie**' *knowing he'll get it*)   It's what we're fighting for.

Alfie *gets it.*

Alfie   It's true enough though. You see the French don't have much of a language.

Squire   Rubbish.

Alfie   Very small vocabulary is French. No more than one hundred words.

Squire   Rubbish!

Alfie   Which is ninety-nine more than Squire here. Most of the Frenchy communication – you'll have noticed this – is done with shrugs. Like this you see.

He shrugs

That means 'You surprise me'.

He shrugs again – identical

That means 'I am not surprised'.

And again.

And that's a question.

Bert   What question?

Alfie   'Are you surprised?' While this one?

Another shrug.

Bert   Am *I* surprised?

Alfie   No, Bert, you're just guessing. That means. (*He gestures to* **Earnshaw**.)

Earnshaw That means 'Come this way to see my sister'.

Alfie You see?

Squire And this. (*Shrugs.*) That's the 'sister' saying I'm not lying with that ugly bastard.

Laughter

Alfie (*shrugs, imitating mademoiselle*) 'He has a gob on him like a robber's dog'

More laughter.

Earnshaw I'm a very good-looking man, I am. (*Pause.*) It's just that people don't notice it.

Quinn *returns to collect the postcards*

Quinn Shit at fighting. Shit at writing. Come on!

*As he takes the card from **Bert**'s hand a cut opens.*

Bert Paper cut, bloody 'ell.

Alfie *takes out a rag and binds his finger.*

Alfie Young Ingham survives the great battle, not a drop o' blood on him anywhere, not even a graze from the wire, and in the process of sending the good news home manages to cut himself open on a postcard.

Earnshaw He might be on to something. Instead of relying on our useless bloody artillery we could all chuck these things at Jerry next time.

Alfie You'll make a staff officer yet, Earny.

Squire You're the one who missed the boat, pal.

Alfie *snorts.*

Squire I'm serious. You played your cards right you could have had 100 men under you by now.

Alfie What do you think's under this lot? (*He nods down to the crater.*)

Conker (*getting it*)   Bloody 'ell.

Quinn (*to* **Bert**)   Come on, give us it.

Bert   There's a bit of blood on the card, I can't send that! That *will* finish my mum off.

Quinn *tries to snatch it but* **Bert** *is too quick and snaps the card away.*

Quinn   Well you'll miss it then, you little twat, 'cause I'm off.

Alfie   That's Corporal Quinn's delightful version of the Last Post.

Bert   Give me another one, corpy.

Quinn   I can't do that. One quick-firer per man.

Alfie *seizes one from* **Quinn***'s packet and gives it to* **Bert**.

Quinn   Oi!

Alfie (*serious*)   You are not telling me that on this day you've got no spares.

Earnshaw *seizes more cards and bolts, leaving* **Quinn** *to chase after him.*

Quinn   Put those back, Earnshaw. (*Pause.*) They belong to the Army.

Scene Two

MANCHESTER, AUGUST 1916.

The Ingham family home. It's the house of an unskilled labourer but shows some touches of culture and learning – a piano perhaps, definitely some books. There's a set of shoes in front of **George** *that he has just been polishing.* **Eliza**, *same age as husband* **George**, *is reading* **Bert***'s Field Service Postcard. She has been folding dried washing.*

George   The men call them 'quick firers' apparently. I suppose it must be a type of gun.

Eliza Well it doesn't say very much.

George It says everything, love. It says he's well.

Eliza It says he's 'quite' well.

George That's good enough for me.

Eliza I'd like to know more.

George Of course you would. So would I. But the important thing is that our son's alive. That's what he's telling us. There's plenty of other families in this town who would love to be told that about their son right now.

Eliza Oh George, he's alive.

She actually clutches the Field Service Post card to her heart.

I knew he'd come through. When they started to print them lists in the evening paper it was as . . .

George Everybody was amazed by how long they were.

Eliza *So* long. I never knew there were that many soldiers from Manchester. That's an awful lot of tears, George. This vale must be sodden with them. But I knew then our boy was fine and I knew he'd find a way to tell us. (*She looks again at the postcard.*) But just a line!

George He'll write a proper letter soon.

Eliza Full of twaddle.

George Aye.

Eliza But the voice of God.

George That too, love. That too.

He resumes polishing.

Eliza We'll need to get knitting soon, me and Agnes, because there'll be a nip coming won't there? Even in France it must get cold. I was thinking a woolly scarf and Agnes can maybe do a pair of gloves.

George   War'll be long over before she's finished them.

Eliza   Oh I hope so.

George   Empires will rise and fall!

Eliza *looks again at the postcard, as if for the first time.*

Eliza   Oh dear.

George   Look at you!

Eliza   Folk are now saying this battle's the last big one.

George   I've stopped listening to that rubbish. Saloon-bar generals. Like that Member of Parliament who came to the Vic and told us all that the Germans were running out of ammunition.

Eliza   Yes he was very sure about that.

George   I knew he were telling a lie.

Eliza   How did you know?

George   You mean apart from the fact his mouth was moving?

Eliza   Well I think we've seen the worst. They can't keep putting men through this kind of ordeal.

Long pause. **George** *stops polishing.*

George   I wonder what he's up to? Right now I mean.

Eliza   He's probably cleaning his boots or something. They love keeping things spotless in the army don't they?

George   Well if a gun's not clean it won't work. (*Pause.*) The winners will be the ones who do the most scrubbing.

Eliza   *They* are never the winners.

George *laughs*

George   He'll be all right will our Bert.

Eliza   I hope so.

George   Oh, I know it.

Eliza   I wish I could be so sure.

George   He will be. He made me a promise, just before he went to France.

Eliza   Bert did?

George   No, General Haig, who do you think?

Eliza   What kind of promise?

George   To come back, safe.

Eliza   Oh George, all lads do that.

George   They do. But there was nothing . . . casual about the promise he made to me.

I wanted him to understand he had to come back. With his heart I wanted him to understand.

Eliza   He has a big heart.

George   And so, he will understand.

Bert *enters singing, followed by* **Alfie**, **Conker**, **Squire**, **Quinn** *and* **Earnshaw** *who carry wooden tables and chairs, as they start to construct a rudimentary tavern.*

Bert   And here's good luck to the pint pot, good luck to the barley mow,
  Jolly good luck to the pint pot, good luck to the barley mow . . .

Scene Three

THE SOMME, 3 OCTOBER 1916

The tavern is a basic affair, behind the lines – nothing more than a drinking place for soldiers.

Bert   Oh the pint pot, half a pint, gill pot, half a gill,
  quarter gill, nipperkin and a round bowl.
  Here's good luck, good luck, good luck to the barley mow.

A waiter delivers bottles of vin blanc ('plonk').

All   Now here's good luck to the half gallon
   Good luck to the Barley Mow'
   Jolly good luck to the half gallon
   Good luck to the Barley Mow'

   Oh the half gallon, pint pot, half a pint, gill pot, half a gill,
   quarter gill, nipperkin and a round bowl
   Here's good luck, good luck, to the barley mow

Bert *is given a bottle of lemonade.*

Bert   Now here's good luck to the gallon
   Good luck to the Barley Mow
   Jolly good luck to the gallon
   Good luck to the Barley Mow

   Oh the gallon, half gallon, pint pot, half a pint, gill pot,
   half a gill, quarter gill, nipperkin and a round bowl
   Here's good luck, good luck, to the barley mow

Alfie *raises a glass and addresses* **Bert**.

Alfie   And I present the mystery of the man who can sing
such a fine toping song and never take a drop himself!

Quinn (*to* **Bert**)   Are you a Quaker or something?

Alfie   No he's a Hindoo.

Squire   *Parlez vous.*

*A waiter enters carrying a bottle of red wine, with a white napkin
around the neck.*

Earnshaw   *Garçon!* Over here.

The waiter heads for **Earnshaw**.

Earnshaw   Now then, boys. There's drinking – as in 'I've
just crawled out of a stone-age cave and I'm thirsty'. And
there's *drinking* – as in 'I'm the product of 3000 years of
Western civilisation and I know that life is a branch of art'.

*The waiter takes more care over this bottle, showing it to **Earnshaw** and even pouring a bit out into the glass for the soldier to taste.*

Earnshaw Oh yes, that's a nice bit o' class is that.

Bert What is it?

Earnshaw Something you couldn't afford and will never miss.

Alfie *slams some coins on the table.*

Alfie Then share it out.

Earnshaw For that much I couldn't even let you smell the cork.

Alfie Give it here.

He pours himself a glass and smells the bouquet.

Quinn *(derisive)* What are you looking for when you do that?

Alfie Summat that doesn't smell of your socks.

Some laughter

Alfie It's become the smell of la belle France for me I'm sad to say.

Quinn You talk out of your arse, Longshaw.

Alfie *(grandstanding)* Unlike your good self who, even in the simple act of asking someone where the shitter is, can move Poet Laureates to bitter tears of frustration.

Quinn You're doing it now.

Earnshaw *(to **Alfie**)* To be fair to the lad you can sometimes sound like you've swallowed a dictionary.

Bert There's nowt wrong in that.

Earnshaw Never said there was, Bert, never said there was.

Bert Better to have knowledge than not.

Earnshaw   I quite agree.

Bert   He used to read Shakespeare at work sometimes. Didn't you, Alfie?

Conker (*not trying to be clever*)   Do you work in the theatre?

Alfie (*looking at* **Earnshaw** *in disbelief*)   No!

Bert   He works in the rail yard like me, Conker.

Squire   I don't understand. Why do you need to know Shakespeare to work in the rail yard?

Earnshaw   This is not the quickest platoon on the Western Front is it?

Bert (*patient*)   He doesn't need to know Shakespeare. He just does. And at dinner time he sometimes gets up on't footplate and becomes Hamlet or something.

Squire (*still puzzled*)   What for?

Bert (*no longer patient*)   To entertain the lads!

Earnshaw   To show off more like.

Alfie   A bit of erudition never went wasted, Earny.

Quinn   There he fucking goes again. What *the fuck* is 'erudition'?

Earnshaw   Summat – I'm guessing here – summat you've probably not got.

Quinn   How the fuck do you know?

Bert (*to* **Quinn**)   It's learning.

Quinn (*defeated*)   Oh.

Alfie   If you can't command words you'll always be someone's slave.

He has his audience and can take his time.

You've all noticed that haven't you?

They have.

Them as push pens also push us. Unfortunately I only figured that one out after I left school – same as Bert here. Talking to old fellas in the yards, amazing what some of them knew. In't it Bert?

Bert Walking encyclopaedias.

Alfie That's right. Little booklets on all sorts they had – on evolution, botany, art, socialism, Carlyle's *History of the French Revolution*. (*Pause.*) Palaeontology. Do you know what that is?

They don't.

Bert It's fossils. Of dinosaurs and stuff.

Alfie Dinosaurs! That's right. Show a bit of interest and these fellas would lend you their booklets. Pleased to. Pages thick wi' engine grease they were. Thumbed, you know, over the years, by God knows how many railmen. (*Pause.*) *Best* men they were. They could talk to the bosses – on the level like – they could talk about wages and conditions because they *knew* about Shakespeare. Not one of 'em were pushed around.

The boys are impressed. A world they don't know. **Bert** *is proud of his mate.*

Alfie *That* is erudition.

Silence . . .

Quinn Well you're still out here aren't you, you cunt?

Laughter from some, embarrassment from others.

Alfie *doesn't join the laughter at first – and when he does join the merriment it's a bit forced.*

Quinn Out here with us and being pushed around!

More laughter

Alfie And I wouldn't be anywhere else!

Earnshaw (*raising his glass*) Good health, lads. May we rest here forgotten for what's left of the war!

Glasses are clinked.

Alfie   You awright, Bert?

Bert   Aye, I'm fine

Alfie   I've got you 'reflecting' have I?

Bert   S'ppose so.

Alfie   Were you thinking about there?

Bert   No, I was thinking about here.

Alfie   What this time?

Bert   Nowt really, I just can't get over how strange the German wire was.

Alfie   How d'you mean?

Bert   Did you not notice? Different to ours, foreign-looking like.

Alfie   It is foreign.

Bert   Different barbs on it though. More . . . barbed somehow.

Alfie   Hey, Bert reckons Fritz's barbed wire is more barbed than ours.

Laughter

Bert   Can't believe nobody else thinks that!

Conker   Those helmets got me. The new ones they wear.

Bert   I agree, Conker. Bloody frightening seeing them close up.

Squire   I liked the old ones, with the spike.

Earnshaw   The Pickelhaube!

Alfie   Smashing word is that.

Squire   They made old Jerry look like a music-hall act, somehow. Less scary anyway.

Conker   That's what I'm saying. The new one's all sort of encased, round here.

Earnshaw   Barbed wire's got more barbs, helmets are more encased. What's up with you, Jennifers?

Bert   See one sideways on and they *do* look made for fighting.

Alfie   Aye, and now *we're* the music-hall turn. Silly little tin bowler against a man *encased* in steel.

Earnshaw (*sings*)   We are Fred Karno's army, the ragtime infantry . . .

Alfie   Oh, bloody 'ell.

The others join in

> We cannot fight, we cannot shoot, what bloody use are we?
> And when we get to Berlin, the Kaiser he will say
> Hoch, hoch, mein Gott! What a bloody rotten lot
> Are the ragtime infantry . . .

Alfie   Hey, Bert. We're going back to the front line.

Bert   What?

Alfie   Two days' time, we're going back.

Bert   How do you know that?

Alfie   I know.

Scene Four

MANCHESTER, 18 DECEMBER 1916

The Ingham home. A little Christmas tree with a few baubles. **Agnes** *is knitting woollen gloves. She's using* **George** *to wind wool, his hands spread out wide with the wool around them.*

Agnes   Tighter, Dad.

George   What?

Agnes   Spread your hands.

There's a knock at the door. From the kitchen **Eliza** *shouts 'I'm coming'.*

George   How many fingers have you done on that glove?

Agnes   How many do you think?

George   Well the correct answer is usually five.

Agnes   That's what I was aiming for.

George   It looks like six from here.

Agnes   Oh well, you can never have too much of a good thing.

George   Bert can always grow another finger I suppose.

Agnes   Aye, it'd be a shame to leave it empty.

George   Be quicker for him to do that than you start again.

Agnes   That wouldn't be a criticism of my knitting would it?

Eliza *enters from the kitchen. She is holding an opened brown envelope.*

George   Well it doesn't measure up to this lady's.

Agnes   That bread smells lovely, Mum.

Eliza *is still as a stone.* **George** *drops the wool.*

George   What is it, love?

Eliza (*stretching her arm and holding out the dreaded envelope*) George.

George   What?

Agnes *rushes forward, takes the letter and reads it.* **Eliza** *just looks at* **George**. **Agnes** *gasps.*

George What does it say?

Eliza What do you think it says?

George Is it from Bert?

Agnes He died of his wounds.

An animal groan from **George**.

Eliza Our boy.

She rushes to **George** *and clutches him.*

Eliza Compose yourself, George.

Big sobs from **George**.

Eliza At least they found his body.

He's inconsolable.

I think most of them are not found.

He detaches himself.

George How do you know that?

She doesn't.

How the hell do you know that?

Agnes Dad!

George They must send him home. I will need to see him.

Scene Five

THE SOMME, 5 OCTOBER 1916

A square, behind the lines. Night-time. Pissing down with rain.
CSM Deakin *is taking the Manchesters through their paces. We see
the platoon come to the end of the drill. Then . . .*

Deakin Private Ingham, Private Longshaw. You are being
attached to Machine Gun Corps, 90th company.

Bert   Sir, are we not going back with the Pals?

Deakin   Is there something wrong with your fucking ears, Ingham?

Bert   No, sir.

Deakin   There must be because I've just told you where you are going.

Bert   Yes, sir, just to say though, sir, we were with the 18th, at Montauban, sir.

Deakin   What do you want me to do? Compose a bloody ballad?

Bert   No, sir. It's just . . .

Deakin   'No sir'! 'No bloody ballad, sir.' You are to report to MGC at seven. Both of you.

Bert/Alfie   Sir!

Deakin *turns his attention to* **Alfie**.

Deakin   You look happy. Do you like the rain?

Alfie   I'm from Manchester, sir.

Deakin *gives* **Alfie** *a good look*.

Deakin   Can you assemble and maintain a Lewis light machine gun?

Alfie   I don't know, sir.

Deakin   What sort of answer is that?

Alfie   It's the truth, sir. I've never tried.

Deakin   Then you can't can you? You will need training.

Alfie   Yes, sir.

Deakin   You need a haircut too, Private.

Alfie   Thank you, sir.

Deakin *misses a beat. Is he being wagged?*

Deakin   Private Ingham here will cut it tonight.

Alfie   He can't do that sir.

Deakin   *What?*

Alfie   *He* needs training sir.

Deakin   Your North Country charm does not work on me, Private Longshaw.

Alfie   That's disappointing, sir, although I'm pleased you think I've got North Country charm.

Deakin   What the hell is wrong with you, man?

Alfie   Nothing, sir. I'm just itchy to get back to the front line.

Deakin   You'll be in my sights, Private, when you do.

He leaves.

Alfie   Christ, I were a bit lippy there weren't I? Surprisingly so, I thought.

Bert   That was daft, Alfie.

Alfie   It was.

Bert   He can hurt you if he wants to.

Alfie   I know.

Bert   Then why the hell do you do it?

Alfie   Awright, Bert, I get your point. No need to become a bore. (*Pause.*) Let's get out of this bloody rain.

They head towards their billet – a ramshackle, semi-derelict barn. The two men start brewing up.

Bert   I hate Deakin.

Alfie   Me too.

Bert   He's a bully, a tyrant and a swearer!

Alfie   In other words a first-class sergeant major! Brave too. I don't mind knowing he's there when we get into a scrape.

Bert (*smiling*)   Not like me.

Alfie   Not true, Bert. Not a streak of cowardice in you.

Bert   Well ta, Alfie!

Alfie   Excess of caution maybe!

Bert *hits him, playfully.*

Alfie   Machine Gun Corps though. Can you imagine what that's like? (*Not enthused.*) Ripping belt after belt into all that soft German flesh?

Bert   They've done it to us.

Alfie   Oh, I know it. (*Pause.*) I just don't fancy doing it to them.

Bert   You've fired your rifle at Jerry.

Alfie   Never.

Bert   Course you bloody have. I've seen you.

Alfie   Never at Jerry though.

Bert   You have. I've been there, watched you do it.

Alfie   When I fire it, I fire it against the war, not the Germans.

Bert   Bollocks you do, Alfie.

Alfie   I do, in mi' own mind.

Bert *looks dumbstruck.* **Alfie**, *for once, struggling for the right word.*

Alfie   It's complicated.

Bert *pours tea into two enamel cups.*

Bert I didn't think they'd send us back so soon. Did you?

Alfie No.

Silence.

Bert Before we came out my dad says to me . . .

Silence.

Alfie What?

Bert He says . . . he told me something, that's all.

Alfie Out with it, Bert.

Bert Just summat that if I'd known, I might not have, you know.

Alfie You 'might not have'?

Bert I probably would have done but I probably *shouldn't* have done.

Alfie This is like trying to drive a nail with a paper hammer.

Bert I'm sorry, Alfie. It's a daft thing really. Forget I said owt.

Alfie You're talking about when we enlisted?

Bert It's something even our Agnes . . . It's nowt.

Silence.

It's perishing isn't it?

Alfie What if we didn't go?

Bert What?

Alfie What if we didn't report to the machine guns tomorrow morning?

Bert Go back with the Pals you mean?

Alfie No. What if we didn't go back at all?

Earnshaw *comes into the shelter*

Earnshaw   Have you seen that can of oil I was carrying?

Rummages, no answer.

Do you know how much they'll fine me if I don't find it?

No answer.

I were carrying it and then next time I looked I wasn't
carrying it any more. Bloody weird. Stand up will you? I
want to see if . . .

Bert   We haven't seen your sodding oil.

Earnshaw   All right chum. No need to bare your teeth.
(*Nods to silent* **Alfie**.) What's up with him?

Alfie *looks at him but doesn't say a thing.*

Earnshaw   Someone finally taken a knife to that tongue?

He leaves.

Bert   Forget I said anything, Alfie.

Alfie   We're all dead men. You know that don't you? Dead
men on reprieve. Me, you, Earnshaw, the lot of us. Sentence
has been passed already.

Bert   I said forget it.

Alfie   Do you remember the day when we marched back?
From the front line?

Bert   Years ago.

Alfie   Three weeks ago. There we were, column of fours,
half of us couldn't keep us heads up, so bloody tired.
Everyone hitching their packs up every twenty yards.

Bert   We must've looked like a right rabble that day.

Alfie   I was thinking 'where's Finchie?', 'where's Stodge?',
'where's Dinger Bell?' And I was also thinking 'who the hell
are you?' to the bloke marching next to me. And the fella on
the other side of me too. (*Nasty.*) 'Who the bloody hell are
you and what you doing in Finchie's place?' It was only later

I understood they was probably thinking the same about me
– and each other. Every one of us a usurper, standing in a
place that some dead man – some friend – used to stand.
There should have been 800 in that company. That's how
we'd started out. 800 men, eighteen officers. Remember the
roll call when we got back to base? How many were counted?

Bert I don't remember.

Alfie Course you fucking remember. There were barely
200. Officers five. (*Pause.*) Bloody amazing! And yet we all
stood there pretending it were normal. I don't know about
you but I never felt so alive, or so damn near dead, as I did
at the moment. Extinction, Bert! We came that close! Them
blokes are never coming back. I don't mind saying that I was
. . . *overpowered* by that thought. The sheer bloody immensity
of it.

Bert *hears his own forbidden thought articulated.*

'Course it doesn't last does it? By the time I'd had some kip,
eaten a meal and took a shave the world had turned a
revolution. I remember staring at the whiskers in that bowl
and I knew that what had happened was behind me. Gone.
Then we sent the postcards home to prove it.

Bert But it hasn't gone has it?

Alfie No.

Bert I never want to face that again.

Alfie Nobody does.

Bert But everybody *does*.

Alfie They don't, Bert. Not everybody.

Bert One or two . . .

Alfie *Lots* of men don't. They're real men, they just don't
go back. The Army don't publicise it of course. They call 'em
'missing'. Or they make up this 'phantom army', y'know the
one. Some big deserter brigade composed of us *and* Jerry

that's meant to inhabit caves and tunnels under no-man's land.

Bert   That's bollocks.

Alfie   That's what I'm saying. It doesn't exist. But both sides, high commands like, find it convenient to spread the idea that it does. Saves them from admitting that thousands of men just skedaddle. Get out of France altogether.

Bert   So where've they gone?

Alfie   Back home – to Prussian farms, Welsh farms, engineering shops, coal mines, wherever they're needed and folk are not too fussy about asking questions. And nobody is, because there's a war on. Some go back and join the navy. They leave here and merge back in somewhere else. You don't hear of it because it's too embarrassing to mention.

Bert   It must be easier for Jerry to go than us.

Alfie   How d'you mean?

Bert   We've got that bloody sea to cross.

Alfie   Shipping doesn't stop just because there's a war on y'know. Likely there's more merchant ships coming and going than ever before.

Bert   What, to England?

Alfie   To Spain, Portugal, Norway, you name it.

Bert   This is . . . mad

Alfie   I wouldn't go without you. I'm not leaving you here.

Bert   What do you mean?

Alfie   Can't be going home with you out here. Imagine facing your mum and dad.

Bert   Stop it, Alfie.

Alfie   'Why did you leave him there?' That's what they'd want to know.

Bert *is silent.*

Alfie   We'd have to go now though.

Bert   Alfie, I can't play this game.

Alfie   It's no bloody game. But it has to be now. Tonight. Before we're sent back to the front. Take every bit of money you got. Ditch everything else.

Bert   We can't do it.

Alfie   What's stopping us?

Bert   The 18th.

Alfie   We're not going back with the 18th. You heard him. We're off to machine guns. Strangers. We owe them nowt.

Bert   They'll be expecting us.

Alfie   They don't even know we exist. If it were the lads who know us I'd go back. I'd have to. But a line's been drawn under that now, hasn't it? No one owes owt to anyone. All debts paid, everything settled – with honour. I'm not opening a new account with folk I don't even know. Nor should you. You've got to think of the people who love you now and what they would want.

Bert   I don't know what they'd want.

Alfie   Course you do. They love you. And I love you too, and that's why you should come with me.

Bert   Where would we head?

Alfie   Dieppe.

Scene Six

MANCHESTER, JANUARY 1917

George *navvying, with two other workmen in their forties or fifties. Unseen by the men* **Agnes**, *wrapped up against the cold, approaches with a basket containing wrapped sandwiches and a tin of hot tea. She watches them for a while, admiring the force and rhythm in the work.*

Agnes   You men work well!

They stop and look at the smartly dressed young woman.

George   Ah, that's my daughter.

The men touch their caps.

Agnes   Too well! All the other crews have stopped for their snap.

George   *We* never bother with food. Unless it's forced down us of course.

He motions and they put down the hammers.

Agnes   Oh, like the suffragettes then!

The two other men take positions out of earshot for a smoke and some food. **George** *pulls up a box for* **Agnes** *to sit on.*

George   Here you are, love.

Agnes *unpacks the sandwiches, tea and a little earthenware pot, which she holds aloft.*

Agnes   Mum's piccalilli!

George   Why are you not at school?

Agnes   We've run out of coal, so they sent everyone home.

George   I wonder if anything will ever return to normal.

Agnes   You mean for us?

George   Well it won't do for us, will it?

Agnes   It will do, Dad. In time.

George   The big bloke. He lost his lad too you know. In Flanders. Six month before our Bert.

Agnes   Do you ever talk about it?

George   No. (*Pause.*) No one does.

Agnes   There's a comfort in knowing though isn't there?

George You mean that . . .

Agnes That so many others understand what you're going through.

George Aye, it's shameful.

Agnes No it's not, Dad.

George It is when you see the swollen regiment of the dead and it makes you feel better.

Agnes Something about grief being shared I suppose.

George Even though nobody says anything.

He laughs a bit.

Agnes It's nice to see you laugh again, Dad.

George I don't think it's real laughter.

Agnes But so many now hate the world because of what they've lost. Has there ever been so much scorn on this island as there is right now?

George Only those who've lost a loved one can hear it.

Agnes It was real laughter.

George I thought he'd come back safe.

Agnes We all did.

George But I knew it.

Silence. She touches his arm.

George You've been lovely, Agnes. Our rock. I know how much you loved your brother.

Agnes Ooh, he'd blush to hear that.

George It's true though isn't it?

Agnes I miss him. Little nuisance. And I hate all this patriotic nonsense. You know I do. But I can't help but feel some pride in what he did, or what he *gave* I suppose.

George   A soldier's death?

Agnes   Yes. I don't mean to say it's 'magnificent'.

George   Because it isn't.

Agnes   But we *can* draw pride can't we?

He squeezes her hand and then uses a spoon to lift some piccalilli on to his sandwich. A chunk or two falls on his work tunic.

George   Dinner medals!

She takes a cloth and rubs at the stains.

Agnes   Yes, you've a full set of them!

Scene Seven

FRANCE, 12 OCTOBER 1916

A tiny cellar of a bombed-out cottage, some miles behind the front line. **Bert** *is huddled in a corner, trying to keep warm, lit by a solitary candle. He has a bucket and is trying to wash himself.* **Alfie***, to* **Bert***'s obvious alarm, bursts in with a bulging sack.*

Bert   Hey! I thought we'd agreed.

Alfie   What?

Bert   The secret knock.

Alfie   Oh yeah. Knock knock.

Bert *shakes his head in disgust.*

Alfie   Or was it knock knock, knockety knock?

Bert   Alfie!

Alfie   All right. Next time.

He opens the sack and a dozen or so tins of bully beef come tumbling out.

Alfie   Look what Alfie's found.

Bert   Found?

Alfie   Nicked!

He takes a penknife to the top of one of the tins and opens it up. He then hands the opened can to **Bert** *who fishes for a spoon and starts to eat greedily.* **Alfie** *meanwhile starts on a second tin.*

Alfie   How is it?

Bert   It's trench food isn't it?

Alfie   Aye, they'd run out of Dover sole.

Bert   Again?

Alfie   It's all right – the quartermaster's on it.

He spits out a piece of gristle.

Ughh, it's like eating an old fella's segs.

Bert *eats on unfazed.*

Bert   How about the rum ration?

Alfie   That's one thing I'll actually miss. Seeing that massive jar of rum coming down the line, like the Ark of the Covenant.

The place suddenly resounds to a series of four or five quick explosions, each one louder than the next. The boys sink a little, as if still in a trench. They are both affected by it.

Bert (*eventually*) Bloody 'ell.

Scene Eight

MANCHESTER, 1918

It's Armistice Day, 11 November – early afternoon. The Ingham home, with **George**, **Eliza** *and* **Agnes**. *Daylight, but not sunny. Street noises coming in – a certain excitement outside.*

Eliza   Draw the curtains, Agnes.

Agnes *looks at* **George**, *who shakes his head ('No need').*

Eliza   I dreaded this day coming.

George   We all did.

Eliza   No doubt there'll have the flags and bunting out.

Agnes   You can't blame them for that, Mum.

George   Peace is peace, love. No one's forgetting. It's relief.

Eliza   It makes you retch.

A knock at the door – unexpected.

Don't answer it.

George   We shouldn't do that.

Agnes *opens the door. A smallish lad of twenty-two in the uniform of a private soldier comes in, wounded arm in a sling. It's* **Robert**, *a neighbour, back from the war.*

George   Robert!

Robert   Mr Ingham.

George   We heard you were back.

Robert   Mrs Ingham. Agnes.

He raises his wounded arm a little.

Aye, been home almost a fortnight.

Agnes   Well, you won't be going back now!

Robert   I've just been in St Peter's. Place has gone barmy. (*Pause.*) But err, I wanted to come round here today, because I know what happened to Bert.

Agnes   That's very thoughtful of you. Isn't it, Mum?

Eliza (*without enthusiasm*)   Yes it is.

Robert You were always very good to me, and I know I lost touch with Bert these past few years, but he was a grand lad. (*Pause.*) He always stuck up for me at school.

Agnes When you *were* in school, Robert.

Robert Aye, that's true I suppose.

George We heard about what had happened to you.

Robert Aye. (*Raising his wounded arm a bit.*) Some of the metal's still in. Always will be they say.

Agnes You were lucky.

Robert Dun't feel like that, but I know what you mean.

Eliza You were always a survivor, Robert.

Robert It were just luck . . . as your Agnes said.

George That's all it is.

Robert He were a good 'un though. Bert. Someone you could rely on in a scrape. (*Pause.*) Like his father.

A moment of electricity between the two men.

I never did thank you, Mr Ingham. Not properly.

No response

You know what I mean don't you?

George You didn't need to thank me, Robert.

Robert I did. And believe me I wanted to at the time but I didn't know how.

George Of course you didn't. And I weren't expecting you to.

Robert I still think about it though. What you did. What you both did. The kindness. (*Pause.*) And I'm sorry Bert's not here now.

Eliza (*sharp*) We all are.

Robert   Of course. I'll leave you now.

George   Show Robert to the door, Agnes.

She does so.

Thank you for coming round, lad.

Scene Nine

FRANCE, AMIENS, 17 OCTOBER 1916

A tailor's shop, nothing too fancy. **Alfie** *is being fitted with a suit by a (non-deferential) French* **Tailor**. **Bert** *waits, already in his suit. New hat on his knee.*

Alfie (*gesturing to his crotch*)   It's a bit tight round here.

Tailor   I can loosen this a little.

He *starts to adjust the pins in the trouser leg.*

Alfie   I can take 'em off you know.

Tailor   Not necessary.

Alfie   Ey' up!

Bert   He likes you!

Alfie   You should know that by now, Bert. The art of being Alfred Longshaw is the art of being irresistible. To every creature who crosses his path.

Tailor   A little more room now?

Alfie   Well I wouldn't throw a party down there, but it'll do the job. (*To* **Bert**.) How do I look?

Bert   As unusual as me.

Tailor   Pantalons, m'sieur.

Alfie *slips off the trousers.*

Alfie   We call 'em kecks.

Tailor *picks up* **Alfie**'s *trousers off the floor.*

Tailor (*to himself, with disgust*)   Les kecks.

Alfie *tries on a couple of hats.*

Tailor   If I can suggest . . .

Alfie   When we want your advice, Beau bloody Brummell, we'll ask for it.

The **Tailor** *gives a Gallic shrug and retreats.*

Bert   You surprise me!

Alfie (*gives his shrug and adopts French accent*)   'Fuck off, you ungrateful Englishman.'

He tries another hat

What about this?

Bert   I have never seen anybody wear anything remotely like that in all the time I've ever been in Manchester.

Alfie   And nor will you.

Bert   Why's that?

Alfie   We're not going to Manchester.

Bert   You what?

Alfie *tilts the hat to perfection. Then calls back the* **Tailor.**

Alfie   This is the one, m'sieur.

Tailor   You will keep the suit on also?

Alfie   I will.

Bert (*pointing the discarded uniforms*)   Can you take these?

Tailor   Monsieur?

Bert   We don't need . . .

Alfie   He means can you wrap 'em up in paper for us?

Tailor *nods and leaves them.*

Bert   Sorry, Alfie, I wasn't thinking.

Alfie   Well start thinking. We'll chuck 'em in the canal when it gets dark.

Bert   You said we weren't going to Manchester.

Alfie   That's right.

Bert   Where *are* we going?

Alfie   We're Americans now.

Scene Ten

MANCHESTER, MAY 1919

The Ingham home. **Conker**, *in civvies, working class and smartly dressed, now twenty-one. He's standing awkwardly erect (the former soldier he is), cap in hand.* **Agnes** *faintly amused by his manner.*

Agnes   Mum and Dad'll be back soon. Is it something you can tell me?

Conker   I'd rather tell it to you all.

Agnes   Well you are mystifying. You'll take a seat though.

He does so

You knew Bert well in France did you, it's just I don't recognise your name, Mr Chestnut.

Conker   I was known out there as 'Conker'. I still am really.

Agnes   Oh I do remember that name in one of his letters. Good name that for a member of the British Army!

Conker   Actually it were named after the tree.

Agnes (*laughing*)   I realise that . . . Conker.

Silence. He clearly isn't going to say much.

Agnes   How long have you been demobbed then?

Conker   This March.

Agnes   That's not bad.

He nods his head in mild agreement.

Agnes   You're not a Manchester lad are you?

Conker   St Helens.

Agnes   Thought I heard a touch of Liverpool there.

Conker   Well it's not really Liverpool.

Agnes (*gentle imitation*)   'It's not really Liverpool'!

He smiles meekly

Agnes   You can relax, Conker, I'm not going to bite you.

He tries, but he's as stiff as before.

Agnes   Though I might do if you don't relax.

Conker   Will they be back soon, your mum and dad?

Agnes (*still amused*)   You're finding this hard aren't you?

Scene Eleven

DIEPPE, 1 NOVEMBER 1916

Bert *and* **Alfie** *shuffle into a small ship's cabin.* **Alfie** *carries an old suitcase which he flings onto a bunk. They both wear their suits. Once in they slam the door. Having made it onto the ship they are both slightly delirious.*

Bert (*tense*)   Jesus! You said it would be easy. (*Breaking into a broad smile.*) It *was* easy.

Alfie   That just shows then doesn't it?

Bert   What?

Alfie   You've got to trust your mate Alfie.

Bert   I do. I wouldn't be here otherwise would I?

Alfie   You wouldn't.

Bert   I wouldn't *be* here.

Alfie   Where would you be?

Bert   Not here.

Alfie   You'd be sitting in a pool of dirty water rubbing whale oil into your sodden feet or you'd be in them rat holes again, listening to that hellish racket.

Bert   I would.

Alfie   That non-stop terrifying clamour.

Bert   Never, ever, to hear another whizz-bang again!

Alfie   I was meaning Sergeant-Major Deakin.

Bert *laughs.*

Alfie   Or you'd be leaning against that parapet waiting for that bloody whistle. (*Pause.*) Or lying in the dirt somewhere . . . asking for your mam.

They both ponder that for a few seconds – not a nice mood change.

Well, Bert, we have forsaken our chance to become landowners in France. France's loss, our gain.

Bert   What now?

Alfie   How do you mean?

Bert   What happens to us now?

Alfie   Nothing. We just sit tight and wait for this beautiful vessel to move.

Bert (*looking around*)   I've never been on a boat before.

Alfie   It's a ship, Bert. We don't call it a boat because it upsets the men who work on it if we call it a boat.

Bert   Why?

Alfie It's a classification thing. Be like calling an officer a man.

Bert I've never been on a *ship* then.

Alfie Well I say you have. Unless they flew you to France.

Bert *laughs*

Alfie Did they fly you to France?

Bert You know they didn't.

Alfie (*posh voice*) 'Ah, Private Ingham, we were wondering if instead of going to France on the ship like the other men you'd prefer to join General Rawlinson in the aeroplane. General Rawlinson has a spare seat and he thought it might be nice if you took it.'

Bert Me with General Rawlinson?

Alfie *makes the sound of a biplane.*

Alfie (*as Rawlinson, as shouting above the engine*) 'Now then, Bert. You don't mind me calling you 'Bert' do you?'

Bert (*through his laughter*) No.

Alfie 'Because we've got to know each other extremely well in this aeroplane haven't we? You see that? (*Two jabs of his arm, pointing downwards.*) Down below there, all those trenches? That's where you'll be fighting. (*Pause.*) It's quite close to where I'm staying actually. (*His thumb points backwards over his shoulder.*) You see that fine chateau? No? Well you would see it in an hour or so's time if you kept on flying back that way. That's where I, err, that's where I'm quartered with my staff. It's lovely. You'd like it, Bert.'

Bert I'm sure I w . . .

Alfie (*as Rawlinson still*) 'Anyway, must drop you off here because you'll be wanting to join your pals. Do you need a parachute? You're sure? Off you go then. Cheerio!'

He makes the noise of a biplane, leaving very quickly.

Bert   I don't remember it happening that way!

Alfie   You've been on a ship then, haven't you?

Bert   That were different though. I mean having our own cabin, wearing our own clothes.

Alfie *nods at his clothes as if to say 'oh yeah?'*

Bert   Well, not us own clothes. But civvies, like. It's like we're millionaires.

Alfie   Oh aye, millionaires. That's us. You should see the state of my wallet.

Bert   You've *got* a wallet?

Alfie   Have I buggery.

Bert   I was wondering that. How we going to eat?

Alfie   Frugally.

Bert   You what?

Alfie *pulls packets of hardtack biscuits and the remaining tins of bully beef from suitcase.*

Alfie   We're going to eat these biscuits and these tins of bully you're so keen on. (*He slaps some coins, mainly copper, some silver, on the table.*) And we can be having one swanky meal on the last night.

Bert   How long will it take, Alfie, before we get to Gothenburg?

Alfie   Might be an idea if you don't call me 'Alfie' any more too. Just till we get to where we're going. (*American accent, convincing.*) 'It's Francis Graydon now. Philadelphia grain merchant. (*Doffing his hat.*) Pleased to make your acquaintance. And you, sir?'

Bert *just smiles.*

Alfie   'Your name, sir, I don't think I caught it.'

Bert (*shy*)   Sam Bostock.

Alfie   'Speak up, Mr Bostock.'

Bert (*terrible American accent*)   'Mr Sam Bostock, also a grain merchant. Phila, Philadale, Phila . . .'

Alfie (*still American*)   ' You know, Mr Bostock, it might be an idea if you say as little as possible. When other folks are around I mean.'

Bert   Why?

Alfie   'You don't sound like a proper American to me.'

Bert   That's because I'm from Manchester.

Alfie   'That's right, Mr Bostock, but the point is to disguise it.'

Bert   I don't know what an American sounds like. I'm just trying to sound like you.

Alfie   'You don't sound a bit like me, Mr Bostock. You sound like me caught up in some devilish agricultural machinery. But you *do* need to sound like me. So do you think you can extricate yourself?'

Bert   I shall try.

Alfie   'Now you must ignore those darned rumours that I learnt my accent from *Huckleberry Finn* and much of my manner by observing travelling players in matinee performances at the Hippodrome on Preston Street.'

Bert laughs (*he knows the Hippodrome*).

Alfie   'For that is a contemptible lie. You know as well as I, that we have spent our entire lives in the great city of *Philadelphia*, in the heart of *Pennsylvania*, where we were raised by our families, who've lived in the United States for four score years and ten.'

Bert   Four score years and ten?

Alfie   'That's the way we Americans say it.'

Bert   How do you know that?

Alfie   'That's the way Abe Lincoln said it.'

Bert   Who?

Alfie (*back to his own accent*)   Yes, you really better let me do the talking.

Bert   I was joking, Alfie. Everyone knows he's the American prime minister.

Alfie *stares at* **Bert** *and shakes his head out of sheer disbelief.*

Bert   No?

Alfie   No, Bert!

Bert   I could be a deaf-mute like that kid we used to know on Hulton Street.

Alfie   No, just be shy. We don't want to over-complicate it. That just makes folk nosey.

Bert   I don't know how you know all this stuff.

Alfie   You'll know the stuff too, Bert, soon enough. More to life than Salford. And there's a helluva lot more to life than Picardy and the bloody River Somme.

Bert   I know that's true an' all.

Alfie   We had no right being there, weren't our fight.

Bert   Well we did sign up!

Alfie   Not for that. (*Pause.*) More to life than that, mate. Just you wait and see. Gothenburg first. They love the English there. Get a bit o'capital. And then America!

Bert   I'm just going to ask you.

Alfie   What?

Bert   So don't get angry.

Alfie   Don't start this again, Bert.

Bert   I don't know whether we should be doing this.

Alfie   We are doing it.

Bert   If we give ourselves up now . . .

*There's a knock on the door. Both men freeze. There's another knock and then a Swedish **Steward** enters. He's surprised to see there is someone inside.*

Steward   Oh, I thought . . .

Two grubby towels are delivered and a block of soap. He also puts up an inventory on the inside of the door.

Steward (*reading from a form*)   Mr Graydon?

Alfie   'That's me.'

Steward   And Mr Bostock.

Alfie   'Yes that's him.'

Steward   English?

Alfie   'American.'

Steward   American!

Bert   'Philadelphia'.

Alfie *shoots him a surprised glance.* (*It's oddly passable.*)

Steward   Well I welcome you both aboard the *Belleville* and on behalf of the captain I wish you a good voyage. My name is Daniel Lindquist and this is my side of the ship. If there's anything you . . .

Alfie   'What time do we set sail, Mr Lindquist?'

Steward   We're still loading but it shouldn't more than thirty minutes now.

He suddenly sees the bully beef tins on the bunk. They see him looking at the tins.

Alfie   'Dog food. We import tinned dog food, to
Philadelphia, thinking of doing so. And these, these are
samples.'

Steward   Yes, sir.

Alfie   'We gonna test it on Fido and Rex. (*Pause – he knows
he has to 'up' it.*) The average American dog is very fussy, Mr
Lindquist. More so than his European counterpart. You
could almost say he has a refined palate.

The **Steward** *looks doubtful, as does* **Bert**.

Alfie   'A very strange thing. An *obscene* thing in my opinion.
But a stubborn commercial fact we have to deal with.'
(*Pause.*)

The **Steward** *picks up a tin.*

Alfie   I don't know why it should be that . . .'

Steward   This is soldiers' food.

Bert *clearly thinks the game is up and is about to say something.*

Alfie   'It is indeed. Or it is at the moment. Very well
discerned, sir, very well discerned. But let me ask you, if I
may. Can you imagine how many excess tons of this 'soldiers'
food' there's gonna be in a couple of months' time?

Steward   In a couple of mo . . .

Alfie   'That's to say when the British Army is billeted in
Berlin and Tommy is dining out in the chop houses of that
venerable – and freshly conquered – town?'

Steward   Ha.

Alfie   'A lot. Mountains of the stuff, no doubt. You'll
probably see it rotting here on the quayside, no good to no
one. But here's my reckoning. What's been good enough for
the British Tommy in Flanders will likely as not be good
enough for Fido and Rex too – damnable fussy as they may
be. That is what myself and Mr Sam Bostock here are

calculating on. It's what we aim to get wealthy on. It's what our noses say.'

Bert 'It's what we . . .'

Alfie (*holding up one of the tins*) 'But I'm sure that Fido and Rex will tell us whether we're right. When we eventually make Philly.'

Steward (*smiles*) You have it all planned, sir.

He makes to leave.

I will see you again once we're clear of the harbour.

Alfie *picks up a bit of silver and hands it to the* **Steward**.

Steward It's not necessary to tip, sir.

Alfie 'We're Americans. It makes us feel better.'

The **Steward** *leaves.* **Alfie** *gestures to the tins of bully.*

Alfie (*throwing the tin to* **Bert**) Put 'em away.

Bert *starts to return them to the case.*

Alfie No, leave them out. But we're not going to touch them.

Bert Did he believe us?

Alfie Did you?

Bert I began to.

Alfie So did he. Fuck me though. Let's just get clear in the water.

Scene Twelve

MANCHESTER, MAY 1919

As in Scene Ten. **George** *and* **Eliza** *enter, surprised to see a stranger in the house.* **Agnes** *gets up and helps* **Eliza** *out of her coat.* **Conker** *leaps to his feet*

Agnes   Mum, Dad, this is Mr Chestnut, an old friend of Bert's from France. 'Conker' from the letters.

George *steps forward to greet* **Conker** *with a handshake.*

George   Very nice to meet you, son.

Conker   You too, sir.

Agnes   At ease, soldier!

An awkward smile from **Conker** *as he tries to relax.*

Agnes   He's got something to say to us all. Haven't you, Conker?

Eliza   Well would he like a cup of tea before he says it?

Conker   No.

All taken slightly aback by his vehemence.

I mean no thank you, Mrs Ingham. I'd feel better if I just said what I've come to say and then . . .

Eliza *takes a seat and motions for* **Conker** *to sit down too.*

Conker   There's not an easy way to say this and I could have gone on dodging it to the end of time because no one would be any the wiser. But it's been preying on me and . . . (*He can't finish the sentence.*)

George   What is it, lad?

Conker   It's your Bert. I was. I was with him on the morning he died.

Eliza   You mean you were next to him when he fell?

Conker   No. I don't mean that.

Eliza   But you spoke to him, before he went . . . (*Uncomfortable saying the jargon.*) 'over the top'?

Conker   Mrs Ingham. He told me his mum and dad would want to know this.

Silence. They are rapt.

He didn't . . . It weren't . . . On 1 July I saw your Bert and he was the bravest of the brave.

Eliza He didn't die on 1 July.

Conker No, I'm just saying I was with him then as well. We got to Montauban which was a long way, turned out it was the longest way, and Bert was very fearless. Not reckless, but he was one of them who was driving the lads forward. Just by doing what he were doing. Sounds a bit funny that doesn't it, but actually it were very calming – to me anyway.

George Well that's nice to know.

Conker I just wanted you both to know that because . . . because . . .

Agnes The Germans didn't kill him did they?

George *and* **Eliza** *look to their daughter, confused, clueless.*

Conker No, they didn't.

Agnes But you were with him the night before he died?

Conker *nods quickly*

Eliza I don't understand. Will someone tell me what's going on?

Conker *looks to* **Agnes**

Agnes Oh God, no.

Still **George** *and* **Eliza** *don't know.*

Agnes Bert was killed by the British Army. (*Pause.*) That's what he's trying to tell us. (*To* **Conker**.) Isn't that right?

A single nod from **Conker**. **George** *now gets it.*

Agnes They executed him.

Eliza It's not true. I have the letter. It says he 'died of gunshot wounds'.

George   He did.

Eliza *breaks down completely.* **Agnes** *takes her out.*

Conker   I am so sorry, Mr Ingham.

George   That's one hell of a thing to tell us, lad. (*Pause.*)
You must have thought bloody hard about whether you
should come here and do that to us.

Conker   I ah . . .

George   You sat with him did you?

Conker   Through some of the night.

George   Well that's something.

Conker   He was very calm, Mr Ingham. Calmer than I was.

George   Hm.

Conker   And we loved him, the Pals I mean. Not just as a
soldier but as a bloke. (*Pause*). And he wanted you to know.

George (*eventually*)   So tell me, what happened?

Scene Thirteen

DIEPPE, 1 NOVEMBER 1916

As Scene Eleven.

Alfie   I thought that was quite passable.

Bert   What was?

Alfie   You know, that accent you put on.

Bert   My American accent?

Alfie   Well I wouldn't go that far.

Bert   I promise you I'll sound like Davy Crockett by the
time . . .

A knock at the cabin door.

Alfie   'Hello?'

The **Steward** *returns.*

Steward   Sir, can you tell me your names and nationality again please?

Alfie   'Mr Graydon and Mr Bostock. Americans.'

Voice of Sergeant Emment   Thank you. I'll take over now.

The **Steward** *leaves the cabin and a uniformed* **Sergeant Emment** *of the British Intelligence Corps enters. Behind him is another soldier with a pistol.*

Emment   Which one is Mr Bostock?

Bert (*eventually*)   Me.

Emment   So you're Mr Graydon?

Alfie *nods, all confidence gone.*

Emment   Shall we do that again? (*This time pitches his eyes above their heads.*)

Which one is Mr Bostock?

Silence.

Mr Graydon?

Silence.

How about you tell me your real names?

Act Two

Scene One

MANCHESTER, 1922

George *in Manchester Reference Library, seated at an empty table. A few other readers diligently scratching away. Eventually a* **Librarian**, *male in his thirties, brings him a copy of the* Report of the War Office Committee of Enquiry into 'Shell Shock' *(published a few months before). He places it in front of* **George**.

Librarian This is it. The 'Southborough Report', His Majesty's Stationery Office, 12 August 1922. You're not the first to look at it actually. I must say it's usual for government reports to simply collect dust, but this one has been surprisingly well thumbed already.

George A lot of public interest?

Librarian Quite so. (*Pause.*) 'Shell-shock', ah, no longer a . . .

George A dirty word?

Librarian Is a way of putting it, yes. You'll see it's organised into evidence, minutes, and then the conclusions.

George I see.

Librarian It's quite straightforward but if you need any assistance finding your way around, do let me know.

The **Librarian** *retreats back to his own corner leaving* **George** *alone. He stares at the document for a while, then tentatively opens it, and carefully turns a page or two. We feel his agony. The thing might as well be hieroglyphics. He closes it and looks around. The reader nearest him gets up and takes his own book back to the librarian, puts on his cap and leaves the library. Silence again. Eventually . . .*

George Sir, I wonder if you *could* help?

The **Librarian** *comes to* **George**.

George   I was thinking, can I take this out of the library, back to my home?

Librarian   This is reference only I'm afraid. You will have to read it here.

Silence, but there's a spell between them.

George   I . . . I can't read.

Librarian   Oh . . . Oh, I see, I . . .

George   My daughter normally helps me. She's a schoolmistress. But, ah, she's not around at the moment and . . .

Librarian   Well I . . .

The two men just look at each other, both embarrassed. Eventually **George** *makes to get up.*

George   No, I'm sorry, I shouldn't have as . . .

Librarian   No, no, it's absolutely fine.

George *heads now towards the exit.*

George   Well thank you and I'll . . .

Librarian   Please wait.

He takes the book.

Come with me. The conclusions. They are very interesting. I can read you those.

He smiles at **George** *encouragingly and* **George** *stops and comes back. But then* **George** *looks at the other readers in the reading room.*

Librarian   I have a private office. We can do it there. And then, perhaps, another time your daughter could come and read the evidence with you.

George   Yes, she could do that. Thank you . . . Thank you.

They head towards another exit with the book.

Scene Two

THE SOMME, 20 NOVEMBER 1916

An empty room in a chateau, behind the lines. **Bert** *and* **Alfie**, *back in military uniform, no weapons. With them is* **Lieutenant Jennings**, *mid-twenties*

Alfie   Court Martial's one below Field Marshal isn't it? That's what my mum'll think. She'll probably be very proud.

Jennings   You might start taking this seriously.

Alfie (*angry*)   I am doing.

A look from **Jennings**.

Alfie   Sir.

Bert   What's going to happen in there, sir?

Jennings   They will read the charge and then they'll hear the witnesses. (*Consulting a note.*) A Sergeant Emment.

Bert   That's the bloke what took us off the boat.

Alfie (*angry*)   The ship!

Jennings   And then you'll have a moment to have your say. You're both clear about that?

Bert   We say 'sorry', sir, and talk about our friends dying . . .

Jennings   Don't overdo that.

Bert   No, sir. And then we say we are not afraid and we would like another chance to fight and prove ourselves.

Jennings   Very good. (*Pause.*) Private Longshaw? You are clear on this?

Alfie   The thing's daft. Sir.

Jennings   I need to know you are clear.

Alfie   On the procedure I am. It sounds very simple. But not the reasons.

Jennings (*harsh*) They are 'simple' too. When you left, you left gaps in the ranks. Those who were more dutiful were then left to fill those gaps.

Alfie Gaps in the ranks were happening all the time, sir. I saw a few develop mi'self.

Jennings You cannot seriously be comparing your own desertion to the field death of your comrades?

Alfie No . . . No. I'm not doing that. I'm just saying that nobody seemed to mind much about them gaps.

Jennings This is repellent for everyone concerned. But those men in that room are not expecting to hear your sob stories. They can be clement, they can be merciful but they will *not* respond to a sob story. Before you go in there, both of you, I want you to understand what exactly is at stake and how best to comport yourselves. It is sensible to be honest, in fact it's your only conceivable policy since the basic facts are established and uncontested. You wobbled, you deserted, you tried with all your might to get away, but now you have recovered your senses and you wish nothing more than to be given a chance to make amends.

Bert I do.

Waiting.

Alfie I do.

Bert We both do, sir.

Jennings But you must fully understand the code you have violated. Desertion, like cowardice, is understood by the army to be an infection. Left untreated it spreads uncontrollably. That's what panic is – a dormant condition in all men, close to the surface, simply waiting for permission to express itself.

Bert We gave that permission?

Jennings   That is what will be said. And you will know from experience how easily panic takes hold of men.

Alfie   We were in Trones Wood, sir.

Jennings   Quite.

Alfie   Happily going forward one minute, blind panic the next. It were a right mash. No Germans to be seen but blokes wild-eyed with fear, and you couldn't put your finger on why.

Bert   Some lads had bolted.

Jennings   And it affected the rest? That is how these men at this tribunal will think.

Alfie   We didn't bolt.

Jennings   Not that day, no.

Alfie   Not any day. It weren't bolting. We made a calm decision.

Jennings   Don't you see that this makes what you did worse? In the heat of a battle things happen. No names, no pack drill. But they will look on what you did as calculated.

Bert (*eventually*)   I don't think they'll kill us though, sir. That'd be a terrible thing to have on their minds.

Jennings   You cannot afford the luxury of thinking like that. The men you are about to see are used to making decisions every day that cause the death of hundreds of soldiers – more, many more. They deal out death warrants all the time. Not lightly, but routinely. Tonight they will sleep the sleep of the just, regardless of what happens.

The penny finally drops for **Bert**.

Bert   Are you saying we have no hope?

Jennings *doesn't know what to say.*

Bert   I want you to tell me!

Jennings If they follow procedure I don't think you have much.

Alfie They'll give us penal servitude won't they?

Bert They won't do that.

Alfie (*angry*) What do you know about it?

Bert They won't do it. You remember when we were new here? We saw them men marching past us – and they were all whistling. And it was Earny who said, 'What's going on, they've got no rifles?' Funny how we all missed that at first. (*Pause.*) They were being marched to military prison. I know you remember it because you said 'lucky buggers', and it were what we were all thinking.

Alfie So?

Bert They were whistling, Alfie. They were happy. (*To* **Jennings**.) There's no way they'll give us owt but a firing squad.

Alfie Bert didn't want to come.

Bert That's not true, sir. I were an equal part of this.

Alfie Well he came because I leaned on him. He's always followed me, even back home. I can be very persuasive.

Jennings Your cause is not entirely hopeless . . .

Alfie It's the art of decimation isn't it?

Jennings Well I don't think it's quite that.

Alfie I do.

Bert What is it?

Alfie Old Roman punishment, Bert. A general called Crassus used it at the time of the slave rebellion. If a legion didn't perform its duty in front of the enemy then a tenth of its number were taken out, chosen at random kind of thing, and the rest had to club them to death. It's an old military tradition.

Jennings   I don't think is helpful.

Alfie   And the army's nowt at all if it's not traditional.

Jennings   You really should shut up.

Alfie   Well if we don't get off with prison, who will shoot us? It'll be the 18th won't it?

No answer.

(*Plaintive.*) Well, won't it?

Bert   The Pals? (*Groaning.*) No-o-o-o.

Alfie   Who else is going to do it, mate? They can't be taking men out of other battalions, just to do this. Make it quick. Deliver a lesson in military ethics at the same time.

Bert   They'd refuse to do it.

Alfie   They'll have to do it, otherwise they'd be next. Disobeying a fucking order. (*Looks to* **Jennings**.) In't that right?

Jennings (*raising his voice*)   You would do well to start composing yourself now.

Alfie *walks away to a corner of the room.*

Jennings (*to* **Bert**)   Why did you leave? (*Pause.*) Was it because your friends were dying?

Bert   Not really.

Jennings   What then?

Bert   It was because nobody talked about it.

He cries. Silence.

Jennings   Let me ask you, and think about this very carefully. Do you think you have shell shock?

Bert   Do you know what Alfie said when someone asked him that?

Jennings *doesn't.*

Bert 'I'm shocked I don't have shell shock.'

Jennings *grunts an approval.*

Bert If I did would it save me?

Jennings Probably not.

Scene Three

MANCHESTER 1923

The Ingham home. **Eliza** *and* **George** *squaring over the kitchen table.*

Eliza Because it was Dieppe, that's why.

George Why is that important?

Eliza You know why it's important.

George You'd feel better if they'd picked him up a few hundred yards behind the front line?

Eliza Yes.

George Wandering around in a daze?

Eliza Yes.

George If only he'd been found shaking like a leaf and skriking like a wee bairn? (*Pause.*) That would make it better for you?

Eliza That you even ask that question shows how little you understand mothers.

George That I ask a . . .

Eliza And especially me.

George I understand *this* mother. I saw the pain she was in.

George *makes for her but she spins away.*

Eliza   You think that pain's gone away?

George *knows it hasn't.*

But Dieppe! And pretending to be someone he wasn't.

George   He didn't do that lightly.

Eliza   How on earth do you know?

George   The real boy had gone by then. The personality shattered. Scooped out. It was an easy thing to become someone else – maybe the natural thing.

Eliza   You speak with such un-won authority.

George   It's called shell shock.

Eliza   I know what it's called. And Bert didn't have it.

George   It's possible he . . .

Eliza   Please do not start that again. You read one book. Or some poor soul who took pity on you had to read it for you – and now you're suddenly . . . (*struggling for the right word*)

George (*trying to lighten the mood*)   The Medical Officer of Health!

Eliza   I don't know why you think this merits a joke. (*Pause.*) Bert was a stowaway George. If you look at the facts straight in the face, as you always say you do, you must know they are humiliating.

George   Why do you find them humiliating?

Eliza   Why do you glory in them?

George   I don't.

Eliza   But you do. Those bitter words you now want on his headstone.

George   They are the truth.

Eliza   You're as bad as they are. It's a glory set of words.

George I'm not glorying anything.

Eliza Of course you are! It's no different to the Army you now say you despise. Well now you *are* the Army.

George I just want his stone to carry the truth.

Eliza Saying those words means you can bare your teeth. Hoist your regimental flag. Ugh, the pride. (*Pause.*) I accept that Bert might have had his reasons for leaving. I know it was out of character in that I know him to be a dutiful boy.

George And a brave one.

Eliza Whatever that means now. (*Pause.*) I can be at peace with what has happened; it doesn't make me love him any less. But I don't want it waved in my face for ever more.

George It's the truth!

Eliza But it's not the *whole* truth. Is it?

Silence.

The whole truth says 'loyal to his friends and kind to strangers'. It says 'a boy with a humorous mind and an abiding love for home'. 'He sang pure like a skylark' – that's what should be on his stone. 'He sang pure like a skylark and when he did so even mucky Salford became radiant.' That's the way he should be remembered. (*Pause.*) Put that on the stone instead.

He shakes his head.

Eliza But your self-righteousness wants something else doesn't it?

George It needs saying, Eliza.

Eliza (*scornful*) 'It *needs* saying!' (*Pause.*) You confuse your own sense of outrage with the world's – and it's that, it's that that authorises your absurd mission.

George You once made a hundred pair of socks for a hundred men you did not know . . .

Eliza   I did that because I was ill with grief.

George   You also did it because you knew those men would be grateful. It was a lovely thing to do. But *it* was an absurd mission as well. And now it's Bert who needs our help.

Eliza   You talk about him like he's still alive.

George   This will keep him alive.

Eliza   With those horrible words? You're not keeping him alive. You're doing the opposite. Every day at sunrise, you will do the opposite.

Silence between them.

You're killing him over and over again.

Scene Four

THE SOMME, 25 NOVEMBER 1916

We see **Bert** *and* **Alfie** *being escorted to a partitioned barn (the barn of their last night). Throughout the upcoming scene they should be present, but as if 'ghosts'.*

The main action is therefore set in the drawing room of a country chateau, twenty miles behind the line – so just a faint rumbling of guns. **Lt Jennings** *is facing a young officers' adjutant,* **Parfitt**.

Parfitt   He's at dinner.

Jennings   I know. But I beg to speak to him. (*Pause.*) You might call it a matter of life and death.

Parfitt *considers, then turns and heads off stage.*

The boys are now settling into their barn and are alone.

Major-General John Shea, *late forties, appears, napkin tucked into his uniform jacket.*

Shea   What the devil is it?

Jennings I am sorry to interrupt your dinner, sir, but I felt I must come.

Shea I've been told nothing, so assume I'm as innocent as your mother.

Jennings Yes, sir.

Shea But not so kind.

Jennings No, sir. Lieutenant Jennings, sir, 18th Manchesters.

Shea *takes a moment, then the penny drops*

Shea Ah, the two boys?

Jennings Yes, sir. I would like to . . .

Shea Open and shut case I should think.

Jennings Well I was hoping it wasn't shut, sir.

Shea Oh it's pretty shut. They're the fellows who became 'Americans' aren't they?

Jennings Yes, sir.

Shea Then I don't quite understand what you expect me to do.

Jennings Be lenient, sir.

Shea Say that again!

Jennings (*less sure*) Be lenient, sir.

Pause, in which **Shea** *examines* **Jennings**. *He softens.*

Shea Well I'll be damned. I almost want to hear you say it a third time. (*Pause.*) Would you care for a drink?

Jennings I am conscious of keeping you from your friends, sir.

Shea What will it be? Brandy, a glass of port?

Jennings I ahh . . .

Shea   Come on, I'm asking you.

Jennings   I like them both sir.

Shea   You can't have both! Parfitt!

The adjutant comes running back in.

Jennings   Then ahh . . .

Shea   You know I'd have thought the lesser of you if you hadn't shown up this evening. *Irregular* as it is.

Jennings   I didn't quite know what the regulations governing this sort of occasion are, sir.

Shea   Quite. So we can invent them ourselves. (*To* **Parfitt**.) Get him a brandy, and one for me.

Parfitt   Yes, sir.

He returns with a tray, holding two glasses and a crystal decanter, and pours.

Shea   And leave the decanter.

Parfitt *does so, then leaves.*

Shea   History of the General Staff in one sentence, eh?

Jennings   I . . . I don't follow, sir.

Shea   'Leave the decanter.' (*He laughs gently.*)

Jennings *tries to laugh too, but it's an awkward pause.*

Shea   Well are you going to speak or are we going to sit here like two dotards?

Jennings   I'm going to speak.

Shea   Good choice.

Jennings   The men know the guilty verdict, sir. They were prepared for that. The facts, as you say, speak for themselves.

Shea   But of course they don't yet know the sentence.

Jennings No, sir.

Shea And nor do you.

Jennings I don't know either, sir.

Shea Good. Everything is at it should be.

Jennings But we hope for mercy.

Pause – no reply from **Shea**.

Jennings Can you tell me the sentence?

Shea Well that would be unusual. (*Pause.*) What do you think of the brandy?

Jennings It's, ah, very fine.

Shea It's actually an Armagnac. Rescued from the Indian Army. 'Stolen' I think it would be fairer to say, along with its many cousins. It came with me when I transferred to the 6th, and again to the 151st, and here it is with me now. Seen action in Peshawar, Bengal, the Transvaal and . . . wherever we are today. France, is it? I think we're down to the last dozen. Maybe this is the baker's. (*He sips.*) As you say, 'very fine'. (*Pause.*) That's the brandy!

Jennings Yes, sir.

Shea But of course you were hoping I'd give you something else.

Jennings I asked if the court has yet decided on the sentence.

Shea It has. (*Pause.*) We expect the Commander-in-Chief to ratify it tomorrow.

Jennings Oh no.

Shea I need hardly add that this conversation isn't taking place. The condemned men must only hear of the sentence eighteen hours before it's exec . . . promulgated.

Jennings Oh no.

Shea   Did you expect anything different?

Jennings   I hoped.

Shea   Of course you did.

Jennings   Was it unanimous?

Shea   That, I can't tell you.

Jennings   Is there any way of finding out.

Shea   Oh, I know the answer, but I am sworn on oath not to say. But I will tell you that the court does not need to be unanimous in order to recommend the death penalty. So it's a fruitless line of enquiry.

Jennings   Don't you find that outrageous, sir?

Shea   My word, this brandy is more potent than I thought.

Jennings   Sir, they have been good soldiers. Physically brave. Keen, actually, until . . .

Shea   Until the moment they decided to run away.

Jennings   Unaccountable . . .

Shea   Unconscionable!

Jennings   That too, sir. But still out of character.

Shea   Yes, we received the submission from their CSM. Ahh.

Jennings   Deakin.

Shea   The one! Boer War, y'know. Stephens knows him. Hard bastard! Said he didn't like one of the boys personally, a mouth on him as wide as the Mersey. Very good that because I understand he's not a native Lancashire man. But he clearly thought the fellow a fine soldier. His friend too. Exemplary conduct throughout the whole of July and August. Saw the younger one with his own eyes entering Montauban. Among the first to get there, he said, in that shattered village.

Jennings I never got that far myself.

Shea Hm.

He pours himself another drink

You know, the army talked about this, back in 1914. The Old Army, that is. What would happen if the conflict lasted more than six months? Officially of course that wasn't going to happen. Over by *you know when*. But unofficially it crossed everybody's mind that a – a 'citizen army', y'know, and all it entailed . . . (*He shakes his head as if to say 'useless'.*) Men plucked from behind desks, from footplates, from lathes, from hillsides. Hard work being a shepherd I'm sure, but not much of a preparation for what we were asking them to do. So the question was how do we deal with the inevitable when it comes? It was bad enough in South Africa for the professionals when the show dragged on, but, well, consider how much worse it is today, for all these civilians and with all this metal flying around. Stuck in trenches for months on end, shitting their pants at dawn and dusk every day because they're always fearing the worst, even if the worst rarely comes. After six months we knew men would wilt – good 'uns included. The question is how to deal with them when it happens. We can't flog them any more like Wellington did. The government put a stop to that. Rightly so. But let me ask you. Tomorrow's orders include Lieutenant Jennings leading an assault on a German position in Mametz Wood. Fifty per cent of your men are going to hang back a little, they always do. We know that. What keeps them going forward, in their own meandering way, is the near certainty they'll be executed if they don't. That's fair I think? (*Meaning a fair summary.*)

Non-committal gesture from **Jennings**.

Shea But tomorrow we forfeit that right. Your men can bolt if they want. The worst that can happen to them is that they'll become pariahs. (*Pause.*) Do you fancy that?

Jennings (*whispered*) No.

Shea   It's the only honest answer, isn't it?

Jennings *looks furious – feeling that he's been played.* **Shea**
finishes his drink and stands up, forcing **Jennings** *up too.*

Shea   Then again the Australians seem to manage. Funny
business isn't it?

The lights go down on **Jennings** *and* **Shea** *and we become aware of*
Bert *and* **Alfie** *again in the barn.*

Scene Five

MANCHESTER, 1924

Sunny day, light pouring in from the street. The back door is open.
Eliza *and* **Agnes** *have glasses of lemonade.* **Eliza** *has an opened*
letter in her hand.

Eliza   You did this for him?

Agnes   I had to.

Eliza   But you say you don't agree with it?

Agnes   You know I don't.

Eliza   Do you never stop to think that your brother has
been in limbo for . . .

Agnes   Eight years.

Eliza   Eight years and we won't let him rest. Six years since
the armistice, five since we were told what really took place –
and we still cannot mourn because your father . . .

Agnes   Mum.

Eliza   And this (*Brandishing the letter again.*) . . . is just
extending the agony. The Imperial War Graves Commission.
They won't change their minds to pacify a deluded old man.

Agnes   I agree.

Eliza   But you've made him sound so . . .

Agnes Reasonable.

Eliza Yes.

Agnes And lucid.

Eliza This might be a time to pity me, Agnes, not poke fun at me.

Agnes Mum, I'm not going to be a shuttle flying between the two of you.

Eliza (*waving the letter*) Clearly not.

Agnes He's entitled to help.

Eliza Even if he's wrong?

George *appears, unseen, at the door in his grimy work clothes. He stays there a moment.*

Agnes He might as well be elegantly wrong.

Eliza It's a silly performance. All you're doing is ministering to his vanity.

Agnes I don't see what's so wrong in that. What harm, really?

Eliza It takes no account of me! That's what's wrong. He's not the only one in this house who's lost a son.

Agnes (*touching* **Eliza**) Mum.

Eliza It's like I don't count.

George *steps in.*

Agnes Oh . . . Hello, Dad.

George *just nods.*

Agnes It's hot out there isn't it? Mum made some lemonade. We've been having some, it's very refreshing.

He nods again.

Would you like some? It's quite cool.

George   Still causing ructions am I?

Eliza   Oh God. There's got to be a word for what you're doing.

George   And what would that be?

Agnes   I'm pouring some lemonade.

Eliza   Well let's start with destroying this family.

George   This family was destroyed the moment that we heard our son was dead.

Eliza   That is typical.

George   Typical of what?

Agnes   It's not typical of anything.

Eliza   Typical of how blind you are.

George   How so?

Eliza   Isn't it obvious?

George   If it were obvious I wouldn't be . . .

Eliza   This family was not destroyed by Bert's dying. You were. Me and Agnes grieved and then carried on. You only began to mend yourself when that lad walked through this door and told us what had happened to our boy. What had *really* happened. (*Pause.*) That was the worst day in my life – worse than the other worst days, George. But I look at my husband now and believe it was one of the best in his.

Agnes   How can you say that, Mum?

Eliza   Well look at him. Look at him! All starchy with purpose. It's made him vigorous again.

George   If that were true why would it be a bad thing?

Eliza   Because it's selfish.

George   Agnes doesn't think it's selfish.

Eliza   But she thinks it's wrong

They both look to her.

Agnes These words – that I've written for you, Dad – they are so overpowering. Can't you see that? They might actually reduce Bert, from all the many things he was to *one thing*.

George I can see that.

Eliza Then why would you wish to pursue it? What point are you making?

George I have no wish to make any point.

Eliza You don't even know why you want these words. For him? (*Pause.*) For you? (*Pause.*) To oppose *them*?

Silence from **George**

Agnes To oppose war?

George (*quiet*) No.

Agnes To oppose the war my brother fought in? To oppose the *way* it was fought?

George All of these things, none of these things.

Eliza Your mind is not clear, George. It's like a jumble sale in there. God love you, it always was. A man without education and a lot of ideas, your thoughts are bound to be like bric-a-brac.

George I've never pretended they were otherwise.

Eliza And yet *these* words, they are are *so* precise.

George *doesn't have the words.*

Agnes What do you think our Bert would say, Dad, if he could read this inscription?

Eliza He'd be ashamed.

George We can't know what he'd feel.

Agnes That's why Mum thinks you should leave the thing bare.

George   And you?

Agnes   Let him be, Dad. I think he'd be embarrassed by the fuss. (*Pause.*) Leave it bare.

George   I can't do that. Unless they stop me I can't do that.

Agnes   But, Dad, they are there for eternity. When you've gone – when we've all gone – the only people reading those words will be strangers. What will they think?

George   Who knows what they'll think?

Eliza   They won't understand.

George   Likely not.

Eliza   And our Bert will be despised.

George *can only shake his head*

Eliza   Agnes has said your inscription would reduce his whole character to a few lines, but I believe it will erase him altogether.

George   He's already been erased. Everything that happened to him in the last month of his life erased him. The court martial, the guilty verdict, everything. It was meant to, I'm sure, because it must be very hard to kill a man in cold blood *who is still there*.

He takes the letter, gently, off **Eliza** *– and gazes at it*

George   I can't read them. You know I can't. But to me these words don't rub him out. They bring him back to life.

He goes back to doorway, filling it. The lights fade.

Scene Six

FRANCE, 1 DECEMBER 1916

A barn some time after midnight. It's divided into two 'rooms'. In one room is **Alfie**, *in the other* **Bert**. *They can't see each other.* **Squire** *appears, nervous, hovering at the door on* **Alfie**'s *side. The light fades on* **Bert**'s *side, leaving him in the dark.*

Alfie Are you going to stay there? Or are you going to come in?

Squire *holds up a bottle of malt and two tin cups.*

Alfie Well I think you've answered that one.

Squire *comes into the barn.* **Alfie** *kicks a box towards him*

Squire How you feeling?

Alfie Ha, decided to cut the small talk then?

Squire *is confused,* **Alfie** *laughs a bit.*

Alfie Don't bother thi'sel, Squire. I'd rather volunteer for a firing squad than volunteer for what you're doing right now.

Squire They drew lots.

Alfie *(straight face but joking)*   For this?

Squire *shakes his head.*

Squire The other.

Alfie So who'll be firing the guns then, the winners or the losers? *(Pause.)* Twelve good men and true, eh? Or is it the twelve Disciples?

Squire No one's happy.

Alfie Yeah, well tell 'em to aim straight. I don't want to be hanging on by a thread.

Silence.

Come on, come on, you're meant to be bucking me up.

He pours two whiskies. They knock 'em back. He pours two more. He knocks it back. Then pours another one.

You know I had a raging toothache earlier and was wondering just before you came in whether to call for the dentist. That's called 'a philosophical dilemma'. Do I want to be improved for execution or should I encourage deterioration?

Squire *looks puzzled.*

Alfie   Lost on you that, i'nt it, Squire? You'd have thought on mi' last night they might have sent me an intellectual.

They both laugh.

Squire   You know Sergeant-Major Deakin tried to save you.

Alfie (*genuinely surprised*)   Did he?

Squire   Bert too.

Alfie   Well Bert shouldn't be going through this.

Squire   Deakin said neither of you should. But he didn't convince 'em. Sure he tried, Alfie, but you know what he's like when he tries to reason summat out. Own worst enemy.

Alfie   Not while I'm still alive he ain't!

A little laughter

The thing about Deakin, he knew we were scum and that scum we'd remain. And that made him honest. No time for 'bringing out the best in us' . . . Thank God. Hate all that.

Squire   I promise you he's cut up right now.

Alfie   Hm.

Squire   Quinn isn't though. Quinn said you should have remembered the Empire. 'The Empire needs us.' It's what he said. Haven't heard anybody say that since we left Manchester.

Alfie   Well I'd have fought for the Empire, if only he'd asked. That'd have been a cause worth dying for. (*Pause.*) Although I was more of a Hippodrome man mi'self. Better class of show. A bit nearer home too. Empire were t'other side of Salford.

Squire   Not that Empire. The real . . .

Alfie (*cutting in*)   Word of advice. Will you take one from Alfie? Last one'll give you.

Squire Aye.

Alfie Never point out the obvious. Guaranteed to cause resentment.

Squire (*smiling*) I'll remember that.

Alfie Quinn's an ignorant bastard too. That's why he's got an opinion about everything. If a man doesn't stay silent occasionally, especially when an argument's taking wing, it means he has no powers of consideration – and therefore nowt he exchanges with you has got the watermark on it, do you know what I mean? I can guarantee you, Quinn knows as much about what happens in the British Empire as a Connemara pig knows about astronomy. You follow Quinn and . . .

Squire Hang on. Is this another last piece of advice?

Alfie You got me there!

He drinks.

Squire I'm wondering . . .

Alfie Don't wonder. You can ask me anything tonight. Tomorrow I'm in another town.

Squire Why did you enlist?

Alfie Why did *you* enlist?

Squire Expectation. Excitement.

Alfie Same with me. Excitement anyway, not sure about expectation. Elder brother's in the ILP, you know. His expectations were different. They *are* different. Bloody socialists.

Silence

Squire Your bro . . .

Alfie Think he thought I let him down when I came back with the King's shilling. 'What do you want to shoot

Germans for? They've nowt against you. Working men *don't* fight working men.' Or some such bollocks. I said 'They've got it in for us in Berlin.' He said he was pretty sure my name hadn't come up at all in the Reichstag. Nor his.

Squire *smiles.*

Alfie   Clever bastard, eh? (*Pause.*)

He offers **Squire** *the bottle, but* **Squire** *declines.* **Alfie** *pours himself another.*

Alfie   Then again, so am I. 'It's slaughter out there isn't it,' he said in his last letter. Take the 's' away I said, that's what it is. Cheers.

Squire   You're an odd 'un, Alfie.

Alfie   He's right though, mi' brother. Germans don't hate us. Not us, like, the common soldier. We've never done 'em a favour so they've never been in our debt – so why should they hate us?

Squire   Is he a conchie, your brother?

Alfie   He's an engineer at Armstrong's so he's reserved. He would be a conchie though. Has it all worked out too. That poster, you know the one with the bloke and his little daughter after it's all over? It doesn't intimidate him. (*Imitating.*) 'What did you do in the Great War, Daddy? Tried to stop the bloody thing, my love.'

Squire *reaches into the breast pocket of his tunic and pulls out a neatly folded newspaper clipping.*

Squire   Mate sent me this from Blighty couple of days back. Made us all laugh. But I thought of you, what you'd say like, if you saw it.

Alfie   What is it?

Squire   It's a clipping from the *Daily Mirror*. November the twenty-second.

Alfie   Let's have a gander.

Squire *hands over the clipping.*

Squire   It's about how British soldiers look when they've been killed in battle.

Alfie *hands it back sharply.*

Alfie   Jesus, Squire, I don't think you've understood the nature of your mission.

Squire   It's not like that. Honest to God.

Alfie *signals for him to read the clipping.*

Squire   By a bloke called W. Beach Thomas, 'war correspondent'.

Alfie   Oh aye, what does the 'W' stand for?

Squire   You'll find out soon enough. This is what he tells them pillocks back home. 'Even as he lies dead on the field' – that's us – 'he looks more quietly faithful, more simply steadfast than others' – that'll be Fritz. 'It's as if he had taken care while he died that there should be no parade in his bearing, no heroics in his posture.' How about that?

Alfie   Funny that because I've got a German newspaper here – the *Munich Evening News*. Also the twenty-second.

He pretends to open a newspaper

(*German accent.*) 'How to Die Like a Proper Soldier': It's a crying shame. Why can't our dead lie like the British Tommy does when he's been shot? It is embarrassing to see our boys saluting when they fall.'

Squire   That's the size of it.

Alfie   You carry that thing around with you do you?

Squire   It's a lucky charm, mate. Can't possibly find mi'sel lying in no man's land with this thing in my pocket telling me how to do it.

*They hear **Bert** singing through the wall and stop. He has a sweet voice. It's an old folk song called 'Searching for Lambs'.*

Bert's Voice   As I walked out one May morning,
  One May morning betime
  I met a maid, from home had strayed
  Just as the sun did shine
  What makes you rise so soon, my dear,
  Your journey to pursue ?
  Your pretty little feet they tread so neat,
  Strike off the morning dew.'

Alfie (*eventually*)   You can't hurt someone with a voice like that.

Squire   It's beautiful.

Alfie   Like a bloody skylark in't he?

*They listen more to **Bert**'s singing.*

Bert's Voice   How gloriously the sun doth shine,
  How pleasant is the air
  I'd rather rest on a true love's breast
  Than any other where.

Alfie   I'm frightened.

Squire   I know you are.

Alfie   I don't want to die.

Bert's Voice   For I am thine and thou art mine,
  No man shall uncomfort thee.
  We'll join our hands in wedded bands
  And married we shall be.

*Lights fade and the singing becomes louder. Light up on **Bert**'s side of the barn as a soldier with a lantern comes in. It's **Conker**. He hears **Bert** singing and thinks about leaving. **Bert** stops and nods him in.*

Conker   They said to come in with a bottle and get you drunk.

Bert   I don't drink.

Conker   That's what I told 'em. They said, 'Well it won't take too long then will it?' *Do* you want a bit?

Bert *shakes his head.*

Bert (*eventually*)   Thanks for coming though, Conker.

Conker   That's all right.

Bert   I thought they might put us with Alfie.

Conker   I don't know why they didn't.

Bert   I do.

A long silence.

Who's gonna be doing the shooting?

Conker   I can't tell you that.

Inhgam   You *won't* tell me that?

Conker   I can't, 'cause I don't know.

Bert   Not you though.

Conker   Not me.

Bert   I won't see 'em will I, cause I'll have the blindfold on, right?

Conker   I think so.

Bert   I wouldn't want to see 'em. I don't suppose they'd want to see me neither. (*Pause.*) I'd give everything to be given another chance and go over the top tomorrow, Conker. I told 'em that too. I said let me atone, actually used that word 'an all, which was a bit surprising because I don't think I've ever used it before in my whole life. But they, ah, they said it were too late for that.

Conker   It's not fair. You should be given another chance.

Bert   I can see why they didn't.

Conker   I can't.

Bert   I'm not yellow though am I?

Conker   Not a bit.

Bert   I just couldn't go back. (*Pause.*) Maybe that's yellow, I don't know.

Silence.

You're never *you* are you? In this war I mean. You're never yourself. Do you feel that? Even now I think, 'There's young Albert Ingham. What's he doing in that cell?' And I felt the same on 1 July. 'What's he doing?' – that's what I was thinking. 'What's Bert doing walking towards them German guns?'

Conker   Silly bugger, eh?

Bert   I weren't fearful though. More, y'know, curious. 'What's he doing?' I mean not 'What's he doing'. I knew what he were doing. But 'What's he doing *that* for?' Dun't he know it's dangerous? When I think about tomorrow morning . . .

Conker   Don't.

Bert   I see it in my mind as you will see it, not as I shall see it. Watching from far away. Alongside you. Funny that in't it?

Conker   I'm gonna have a drink.

He reaches for the bottle.

Bert   Aye, go on.

Conker *takes a stiff drink.*

Conker   No more dark stuff, Bert. It can't do you any good.

Bert   Fair dos (*Pause.*) When was the first time you saw a dead man?

Conker   Bloody 'ell!

Bert *laughs*.

Bert   Come on, I'd like to know.

Conker   I can't remember.

Bert   Out here though?

Conker   Out here.

Bert   Me too. I saw a dead man first week here. Way behind the front line, we hadn't been in France two minute. Bloke had been hit by a stray, a Fifty-Niner probably, but I didn't know that then. Big bloke he was. I were looking straight at him as we marched by. Whole company did. He had a look on his face like he'd just forgotten to do something important. It was the strangest thing. (*Pause.*) As long as I could, I looked at him. Trying to find some clue, you know? Why had it happened to him and not someone else? Thought he might show me that secret.

Conker   I know what you mean.

Bert   Not a single bloke who's figured it out yet.

Conker   It's chance in't it? Everyone knows it. Save yourself an headache if you accept that.

Bert   Aye, and yet, somehow, I feel like I was always heading to this place. (*Pause.*) Even though it's not me!

Silence.

I think mi' mum'll take it bad. Well I know she will. Mi' own fault really. Whenever I wrote home I kept saying what fun it all was.

Conker   We all do that.

Bert   Exactly. So it'll just make her even more confused. 'Why did he run away? He said he was having fun like the other lads.'

Conker   She might never find out, Bert. (*Pause.*) On the certificates they just put . . .

Bert (*angry*)   I know what they put.

Silence.

Sorry, Conker.

Conker   That's awright.

Bert   And mi' dad too. He doesn't read, you know. Never learnt his letters so if it says owt in the paper he won't . . . I suppose other people'd tell him though wouldn't they? Bound to eventually. He's a very proud man. It'll be like hitting him with a hammer. Bad enough losing your son isn't it, but . . .

Conker   Are you sure you don't want a drink?

Bert *shakes his head.*

Bert   Are you cold?

Conker   Getting cold again isn't it?

Bert   Aye, it's the start of a snap I think. I reckon it'll be setting in for good soon, winter like.

Conker   Chapped hands, frozen toes.

Bert   More running noses than standing pricks!

Conker   Balls retreating quicker than the Surreys!

Bert *laughs gently.*

Bert   Things might calm down a little for you though.

Conker   That'd be nice.

Bert   You might get to go home for a bit.

Conker   I could be having that.

Silence.

Bert   Mi' dad . . . Can I just talk about mi' dad?

Conker   'Course you can.

Bert He's a bit unusual you know. I don't mean odd, but just not like the other fathers round where we lived. Somebody, somebody who knew their stuff like, once called him a 'village Hampden'. I hadn't a clue what it meant. Do you know?

Conker *shakes his head.*

Bert It comes from a poem by a man called Gray. My sister showed it me. Lovely poem, it is, called 'Elegy in a Churchyard', something like that. No, don't worry I'm not going to get morbid. It's about wasted lives you know, lives never given a chance to blossom. And the 'village Hampden' is one of them I suppose – 'some village Hampden, that with dauntless breast / Some tyrant of the fields withstood'. I read it and . . . All that talent, never . . . (*He holds back to tears and changes tack.*). He never hit us, Dad, which *was* unusual on Majestic Street. There were always some kid getting a hiding. That many squeals when we were nippers it sounded like a farmyard. Cross the back there was this poor lad called Robert, sort of my pal, y'know, not very lovable though because he were never cleaned, but he had belt marks up and down his legs. Like sailors' tatoos they were, always there, like. As soon as one had gone another appeared. One night he were taking a thrashing from his da' so bad that we just sat there in silence in our own house listening to it, not able to look at each other. Through what? Not pity. Shame I suppose. (*Pause.*) I could feel the rage rising in my dad. He didn't say owt. He were just very still but I knew he were in turmoil. Then he got up out of his seat, still didn't say a word and the door went. We knew where he were going. Anyway the sound stopped. Such silence, like when the guns stop here, y'know. And in a minute he comes back with Robert and Mum takes him in that night and protects him, looks after him like. I remember me and my sister were being extra nice to him, and Mum give him a proper wash – must have been first real scrub he'd had in years. Then morning comes. I remember it so well. It were a perfect summer morning. Salford glory! Must have been a Sunday I suppose

so there were no smoke in the sky to spoil it. Bloke had
sobered up and he comes round, and he were no longer
angry, more embarrassed you know at taking up the strap.
And he's at our doorstep to collect Robert, trying to sound
all normal, as if nowt much had happened. 'Lovely
morning,' he says, 'what have we done to deserve this?' And
Dad just looks at him and says 'I know what I've done.
What've *you* done?' I looked at mi' dad then and I knew he
were a big man. And I knew the other fella knew it too. He
were filling the doorway, mi' dad, but it were like his spirit
were filling the whole street – the whole universe. (*Laughter.*)
Same thing, I suppose. (*Serious.*) He was a giant in my eyes.
(*Pause.*) I think he should know what has happened to me.

This registers with **Conker**, *but he doesn't say anything*.

Bert   It's like I can feel the universe slipping away from me.

He makes a grasping motion.

Nowt to hold on to. It's going and I'm staying still, like.

Conker *wipes a tear resentfully, vigorously, away from his eye*

Bert   Don't cry, you bastard. Otherwise I'll sing again. And
that'll make you bloody cry.

Conker *cannot say a thing.*

Bert   Would you mind leaving, Conker?

Conker   Are you sure?

Bert   Aye, I'm sure.

Conker   If you want I will tell your mum and dad.

Bert (*thinks*)   Make it sound like . . .

He can't complete the thought and instead spreads his hands.

Conker   I know what I feel, so I'll 'em.

Bert *holds up the bottle.*

Bert   Take it with you, and share it with the lads

Conker *retreats to the door.*

Conker I'll always remember you, mate.

Bert (*a little smile*) You too.

Darkness. A knocking on the partition wall.

Alfie Bert? Bert? Can you hear me.

Bert I can, Alfie.

Alfie It's first light isn't it?

Bert I think so.

Alfie It should be last light. Shouldn't let us glimpse the day and then take it away. Don't show us what might have been. That in't fair. It should be last light. Let the world die with us.

Bert They do it 'cause we're young. They're mocking us.

Alfie I am so frightened.

Bert Don't be frightened.

Alfie You'll be with me tomorrow?

Bert I'll be with you.

Alfie Don't leave me please.

Bert You'll feel me there.

Again, **Alfie** *and* **Bert** *should remain on stage, partitioned and shadowed as . . .*

Scene Seven

LONDON, IMPERIAL WAR GRAVES COMMISSION, 1925

. . . we pick up the thread of the Prologue with **Max**, **George** *and* **Agnes** *now in Henderson's office. It's functional, a desk, a lamp, three chairs. Behind the desk is a long chest of draws suggesting hundreds of thousands of index cards inside – a draw lies semi-open so we can see some of the cards.* **Max** *notices this and discreetly closes it.*

The encounter should feel awkward because they will talk about things that didn't have a public language in 1925, and wouldn't do so until many decades later.

Max   Don't sit there, Mr Ingham. Sit here.

He motions to the comfortable chair next to his desk. **George** *obeys.* **Max** *carries another seat towards his desk.*

Max   And madam, please.

Agnes *sits.* **Max** *takes his own seat at the opposite side of the desk.*

Max   It's most interesting to meet you at last. Put a face to all those letters.

George   This is Agnes, my daughter. Bert's sister.

Max   Max Henderson.

They shake hands

George   She's a schoolteacher.

Max *nods.*

George   She wrote the letters for me . . . It's why they are so well spoken.

Max   Indeed they are.

Agnes   We were surprised by the nature of the building, Mr Henderson.

Max   In what way?

Agnes   So modest.

George   I imagined the Imperial War Graves Commission to be living in a more handsome place than this.

Max   It's serviceable. I think that's what you might call it. The grandeur, of course, is in France and Belgium. And that's how it should be, should it not?

Agnes   Oh yes.

Max Commemoration has not been a straightforward thing, politically I mean, as I think you must be aware.

Agnes Most people we know would quite like their lads' remains to be repatriated.

Max That's gracefully understated, Miss Ingham. Because it's actually a very strong feeling that people have. A *natural* feeling too perhaps.

Agnes We want our loved ones next to us. We always have done.

Max We always have done. (*Pause.*) But to accomplish that today . . .

Agnes It's practically impossible.

Max Yes.

Agnes *So many.*

Max *nods forlornly.*

Agnes Much easier to ship headstones over there than . . .

Max Than the other way round. As it were.

Agnes As it were.

Max But I do believe, in the end, our solution is not just the right one; it is the magnificent one. When you see our work in France, the cemeteries are . . . they are unbelievably moving.

George Once the trees grow they'll be right enough.

Max They will, Mr Ingham.

George They said it was an 'unusual' request.

The abruptness slightly throws **Max.**

George That was the first man what wrote back to us.

Max (*getting it*) Ah.

George   He said that.

Max   Well, actually, it's not unusual. (*Pause.*) It's unique.

George *is perplexed.*

Agnes (*quietly to* **George**.)   The only one.

Max   We have fielded no other request like yours, or anything like yours, Mr Ingham.

He waits for a reaction that never comes.

Are you surprised by that?

George   I am, sir.

Max   You see I'm not. Nor is anyone else I've spoken to here. I daresay your daughter isn't either.

Agnes *puts her head down. She won't re-open an old argument in front of a stranger.*

Max   What you're asking for, Mr Ingham, is . . . it's amazing.

Silence. **George** *holds the other man's eye.*

Max   'Shot at Dawn'.

The words are left hanging in the room, like gunfire. But **George** *does not flinch.*

George (*eventually*)   'Shot at Dawn. One of the First to Enlist. A Worthy Son of his Father.'

Max (*grasps a sheaf of letters from the desk*)   Yes, you've never wavered on that. But you ah . . . (*He turns to* **Agnes**.) You see our difficulty.

George   Difficult things are not impossible things.

Max   Not always, that is true. It would be hypocritical for me to, especially in this building, to say that. But you know, it took a long time, a good deal of dispute, before the Commission agreed to place deserters alongside – I am being frank here, Mr Ingham, because I do not like hiding behind euphemism . . .

Agnes There's been too much of that.

Max Quite so.

Agnes No one wants euphemism. Least of all our dad.

(**George** *doesn't know the word 'euphemism' but senses something important has been said. He maintains his sturdy gaze.*)

Max Evidently. (*Pause.*) But it took a lot of soul-searching, and a lot of politics too, before the War Office decided we would bury those men executed by Field General Court Martial alongside the ordinary dead – the 'glorious dead'.

Agnes That was a . . .

Max In my opinion when that decision was made it was a . . . a triumph.

Neither **George** *nor* **Agnes** *was expecting that.*

Max I was very pleased because there is an important principle about equality involved in that decision. Men and officers buried in the same cemetery, no distinctions. Christians, Jews, Muslims, atheists even, together. Men, like your son, buried alongside those who did their duty to the bitter end. Each headstone the same shape, the same size, none bigger, none smaller. Each grave tended with the *same* care, with no prejudice.

George That is the human way to do it.

Max It is. But it was still not an easy decision to make – and for 'human' reasons too. Being 'human' is, we have all discovered in the last ten years, not as straightforward as perhaps we once thought.

George It should be *more* straightforward.

Max Well, in one sense . . .

George In *every* sense, Mr Henderson. Otherwise we've learnt nothing.

Max   Well . . . perhaps. But now what you want – these words – 'Shot at Dawn', on his headstone. That is to re-open all the arguments. It is to revive all that bitterness and to pick once again at all those enraged sores. (*Pause.*) Don't you see?

George   I cannot be made responsible for any other man's gravestone.

Max   That's not my . . .

George   I am not concerned about your policy either. I just know what ought to be said on my son's gravestone. And that is the truth.

Max   But the truth *will* hurt you. It cannot be otherwise. This is why there is no reference to your son's execution on his headstone. And the same is true of the man next to him.

Agnes   Alfred Longshaw.

Max   Of course. They were friends.

Agnes   They enlisted together.

Max   And they deserted together.

George   They did both together.

Max   We don't . . .

George   September 1914. That's when they enlisted.

Max   I'm acquainted with that.

George   October 1916. That's when they deserted. After three weeks solid in the front line.

Max   I'm familiar with his history.

George   And they were shot together and now they lie together, like the Pals they are. (*Pause.*) Did you fight, Mr Henderson?

Max   I did. I was *on* the Somme. The same as your boy.

George   Did you never see men who were scared?

Max All the time.

George But never men who ran away?

Max Most who were scared remained where they were.

George In Manchester Reference Library I was shown the Report.

Max The Report . . .?

George The shell-shock one.

Max Ha, the 'Southborough Enquiry'. You read that?

George Well I . . .

Agnes Dad has been very diligent.

Max It is, ah, a rather confused document.

George In places, I'll grant.

Max What it gives to those stricken men with one hand it takes away with the other.

George Better to be uncertain though than to be wrong.

Max But I'm not . . .

George One man in there, a general, talks of breaking in men like horses.

Max (*a slight laugh*) Lord Gort – Grenadier Guards.

George That's him.

Max A very brave soldier.

George I can understand a man saying such a thing in 1914, *just about*. Although men are not animals even though other men, like him, cannot see it. But in 1922? After everything that's been learnt? No, that's wrong.

Max I don't entirely follow.

George After what we've come to know about the damage that was done in there.

He taps the side of his head several times.

To legions of men – including my lad.

Max   But *your* boy was not suffering from shell shock.

George   How do you know?

Max   Because he was showing absolutely no signs of it. A medical officer testified to this. None at all.

George   But what's known now is not what was known then. 'Mutilation' of a friend, *'annalation'* of a friend.

Agnes   'Annihilation'.

George   'Annihilation', that's right. These are not words I normally use but they were in that Report. Our Bert saw with his own eyes friends who'd been 'mutilated', 'annihilated'. (*Pause.*) Saw them with his own eyes.

Agnes   Dad.

George   That Report says these things could have an effect on a man's mind. Not make him think straight. (*Pause.*) It also says all men may be cowards one day and brave the next.

Max   As I say it is confused.

George   That's not confused!

Max   But the facts of your son's case, Mr Ingham – and of Alfred Longshaw's too. They left the front line altogether – quite deliberately. And they had no intention of going back.

George   My lad – and his pal – were in the 18th Manchesters, and I have been told they went as far as anyone in that July month.

Max   They did. It's a recorded fact.

George   They were waiting for others to catch up. Place called Montybon.

Max   Montauban.

George   But nobody did.

Silence.

They fought as fiercely as anyone on the Somme field and they waited for help so that they could push on again. But that help never came. The others had gone backwards. As a *big group* they'd gone backwards.

Max   There are many reasons why . . . why the offensive on the Somme failed to reach its objectives.

Agnes   Might we not look to the stupidity of the generals for that?

Max   Well that's an opinion . . .

Agnes   And then they did it all over again the following year at Passchendaele. An encore you might say, except the man in charge thought it was a premiere.

Max   You mean General Haig.

Agnes *(bitter)*   Of course I do.

Max   Well he has . . .

Agnes   I understand he was punished with an earldom.

Max   But surely we are not here to discuss strategy.

Silence.

George   You think it's a shameful thing?

Max   I beg your pardon.

George   You said the truth about my son's execution would hurt me which can only mean you think I'm ashamed. But it is you who are ashamed of what you did to my son. That is why you object to my request.

Max   No, Mr Ingham, that's simply not true. We do not refer to the manner of his death, his execution, not because we wish to cover up our own shame – the state feels no shame – still less because of any miscarriage of justice.

Reaction – **Agnes** *reaches across and squeezes her father's hand.*

Max   We do it to *spare you.* (*He holds the letters again.*) Your words, if put on your boy's headstone, will scandalise public opinion.

George   Do you think I care? Do you?

Max *makes a mollifying gesture then gets up. This is very difficult for him.*

Max   You say you are beyond all that – that you cannot be touched by another's reproach. And, meeting you now, I do believe you. But this is not a question that can only be settled by you. Others must have a say. You asked me if I fought and I told you I did. I will tell you now that there are things that are known by those who fought that will never be known by the home population. You will not find in any cemetery in France or Belgium, or any other theatre, any reference to how a man died while fighting for his country. None at all. Can you imagine if we did refer to these things? 'Killed assaulting a German battery.' 'Killed by his own Mills bomb.' 'Killed in no man's land while rescuing a wounded comrade.' 'Killed while running away.' 'Killed by a sniper.' 'Killed while trying to rob a booby-trapped body.' 'Killed by German gas.' 'Killed by our own gas.' You see? The whole thing would be invidious.

Silence.

Do you see?

George   I am not looking beyond my own son.

Agnes   Do you think it looks like an accusation? Is that your real objection?

Max (*gently*)   Well doesn't it?

George   It *is* an accusation.

Agnes   Dad!

George How could it not be? But that's not my purpose.
I'm not arguing against your right to kill him now. I have my
own thoughts, but I won't say a word more on that. I have
exhausted myself on that. She knows it. (*Pause.*) My intention
is not to point a finger, or start a fight. My boy lost his fight.
For ever. But I will have the truth. (*Pause.*) In stone.

Silence again.

Max I've never met a man like you before, Mr Ingham.
You astound me. But you impress me too, even though I
believe you to be wrong.

George You won't give me what I want. I know that. (*He
circles his finger.*) This building won't give me what I want. If I
was young enough I would go out to France myself, with my
tools, and put the words on, myself. Count yourself
fortunate you are dealing with a man past his best.

He gets up to leave.

Agnes Dad!

She starts to follow him but he holds up an arm and she stops.

Agnes *and* **Max** *remain on stage as . . .*

Scene Eight

FRANCE, 7.30 A.M., 1 DECEMBER 1916

. . . the first faint daylight enters the barn. Four soldiers come for
Alfie *and* **Bert.** *Both men are ready,* **Bert** *sitting on his stool,* **Alfie**
standing and face pressed against the partition wall.

Alfie No. No. Please, no.

*The soldiers set about their work efficiently, tying the men's hands
behind their back.* **Bert** *does not resist,* **Alfie** *does and has to be
roughly treated.*

Alfie It's too soon. I don't. I don't want to.

The soldiers then produce sacks which they put over the men's heads and tie at the neck. Again, **Bert** *lets this happen and* **Alfie** *resists the best he can and kicks out.*

Alfie   Bert! Bert! Are they putting a bag over your head?

Bert   Let them do it, Alfie.

The sack is slipped over **Alfie***'s tossing head and drawn tight.*

Alfie (*hysterical*)   Let me just see. Once more. Please.

Bert   Alfie! I'll be with you soon! We'll say goodbye.

He is marched out. **Alfie** *has to be dragged.*

Scene Nine

IMPERIAL WAR GRAVES COMMISSION

Agnes *and* **Max** *are alone now.*

Agnes   He has always been an obstinate man.

Max   It's a virtue I think. Especially in the older ones.

Agnes   I'm surprised you say that. I think we have deferred to the old for too long and . . .

Max   It is the young who have paid the price?

Agnes   Well haven't they?

He shakes his head. Perhaps she's right.

I've still got the gloves I was knitting him. One and a half gloves. I can't seem to throw them away.

Max   I think you do not want what your father wants?

Agnes   He will not be moved on this.

Max   Because you've tried.

Agnes   It has broken my mother's heart. And I . . . well I think Bert should be allowed to join the rest, to slide back into anonymity. That was the condition he was in when he enlisted in 1914, regardless of the fact that he thought – we all thought – he was the king of England when he first came home in the uniform. But, no, he was anonymous then, and should be now. It's in the anonymous mass, after all, where the honour lies and where bravery can be spoken of without blushing. And Bert was brave. He didn't wait to be fetched. He should now join the others.

Max Your father knows these arguments?

Agnes Intimately! There wasn't a single thing you told him today that he hasn't wrestled with for years now.

Max Miss Ingham, I have made a decision. I was hoping your father might be persuaded to see the alternative point of view, to appreciate why what he wants is a bad idea that can only harm him and, I believe, the reputation of your brother.

She gently nods, knowing the truth.

But we *will* permit your brother's headstone to carry the legend your father desires.

She gasps in disbelief

I hope still he will think on what has been said today and will yet change his mind. But I am beginning to understand that such a thing is likely never to happen. And so, reluctantly, it will be done. I am sorry if I've contributed to your own defeat.

Agnes Oh thank you, thank you.

Scene Ten

FRANCE, 8.00 A.M., 1 DECEMBER 1916

. . . two 4 foot wooden stakes are planted in the ground. A single drum beat. **Bert** *and* **Alfie***, both with the sacks over the heads, are marched in by two armed soldiers. They are taken to the stakes. Two more soldiers come in with rope and tie the arms of the men behind the stakes. Two white squares are produced and put over the hearts of the two men. At this point* **Alfie** *starts to lose his nerve again.*

Bert   Alfie . . . Alfie!

Alfie   Bert!

He starts shaking and groaning. Dawn is now breaking. The tempo of the drumming gets quicker.

Bert   I am with you, Alfie.

Alfie   Thank you. Thank you.

Bert   For ever.

The 'For ever' turns into a battle cry (like 'Lancashire' in the Prologue). A whistle, as also in the Prologue. The volley of rifle fire comes from the audience.

To black. We hear the sound of a party.

Epilogue

MANCHESTER, SEPTEMBER 1914

The Ingham home. **George** *is on his own, deep in thought; the party is next door. Eventually a door opens and* **Bert** *steps in, wearing his new army uniform.*

Bert What is it dad?

George Sorry to drag you away from your party lad.

Bert Agnes is teaching me how to march.

George So you're set on standing out from the rest of the army are you?

Bert Are you saying she dun't know what she's doing?

George Agnes knows how to dance. She does *not* know how to march!

Bert She says that after she's finished with me I'll be the best marcher in the army.

George (*imitating* **Agnes**) 'Look at them! They're all out of step 'part from our Bert!'

Bert *laughs.*

They're very proud of you son. You can see that.

Bert (*standing straight, a little ironically*) I'm proud of mi'self.

George And rightly so. (*Pause.*) Rightly so.

Bert Alfie reckons we'll be out in Belgium by the end of the month.

George Does he?

Bert He thinks we'll attack the Kaiser from the port of Antwerp.

George He'll be a General soon that young fella.

Bert *laughs, a bit chastened.*

Bert   He's just keen to get out there, that's all.

George   Hm . . . Are you?

Bert   I didn't sign up to stay here.

George   Well I suppose you didn't.

Bert   You think it's wrong?

George   What?

Bert   Me going.

George   No, not if that's what you honestly want.

Bert   The war then?

George   Politics isn't my thing.

Bert   But?

George   But it looks like a Kings' fight to me.

Pause – perhaps it looks like a 'Kings' fight' to **Bert** *too.*

Bert   I still want to go and see what it's like. Do you understand that dad?

George   I do.

Bert   What is it?

George (*Eventually.*)   There was a little boy called James once – Jim your mum called him. He was a very smiley wee fella, utterly delighted with the world and it was impossible to look at him and not be delighted with it yourself. That's a gift, you see. In a child or a grown man or woman. He didn't live past three months, didn't Jim – something wrong with his blood. He was loved and his leaving was a deep, ferocious, sorrow.

Silence.

Bert   Is he . . .

George Your mother wasn't sure she wanted another child after that and when Agnes came we must have watched over her like guards. I thought it was love but really it was anxiety. Maybe that's a form of love. Every time Agnes fell poorly we mounted a vigil. But she blazed a trail for you and showed it could be done. And then you came and ha! . . . Have you ever even had a sniffle Bert?

Bert Why have you never told me?

George A constitution of an ox!

Bert Does Agnes know?

George There's no reason to tell her.

Bert But you're telling me.

George This family couldn't stand another lost child, Bert. You're going and no one will stop you. But please. Hang on to life lad and don't let anyone take it away from you easy. Just . . . Be careful. Think of your mum. And live.

Agnes *bursts in – bringing party sounds with her. She grabs* **Bert** *by the hand.*

Agnes Come sing for us, Bert.

She stops, sensitive to the mood.

Will you come, Bert? We would like to hear you sing.

Bert Dad?

George Go on, lad. On your way. I'll sit here awhile.

Agnes *leads* **Bert** *out leaving* **George** *alone. But from next door we hear* **Bert** *and others sing 'Hail the Smiling Morn'.* **George** *listens for a while, then breaks into a smile and joins the singing.*

Hail smiling morn, smiling morn
That tips the hills with gold, that tips the hills with gold
And whose rosy fingers ope wide the gates of day,
And whose rosy fingers ope wide the gates of day, the gates of day
Hail! Hail! Hail!

Bloomsbury Methuen Drama Modern Plays

include work by

Bola Agbaje	Robert Holman
Edward Albee	Caroline Horton
Davey Anderson	Terry Johnson
Jean Anouilh	Sarah Kane
John Arden	Barrie Keeffe
Peter Barnes	Doug Lucie
Sebastian Barry	Anders Lustgarten
Alistair Beaton	David Mamet
Brendan Behan	Patrick Marber
Edward Bond	Martin McDonagh
William Boyd	Arthur Miller
Bertolt Brecht	D. C. Moore
Howard Brenton	Tom Murphy
Amelia Bullmore	Phyllis Nagy
Anthony Burgess	Anthony Neilson
Leo Butler	Peter Nichols
Jim Cartwright	Joe Orton
Lolita Chakrabarti	Joe Penhall
Caryl Churchill	Luigi Pirandello
Lucinda Coxon	Stephen Poliakoff
Curious Directive	Lucy Prebble
Nick Darke	Peter Quilter
Shelagh Delaney	Mark Ravenhill
Ishy Din	Philip Ridley
Claire Dowie	Willy Russell
David Edgar	Jean-Paul Sartre
David Eldridge	Sam Shepard
Dario Fo	Martin Sherman
Michael Frayn	Wole Soyinka
John Godber	Simon Stephens
Paul Godfrey	Peter Straughan
James Graham	Kate Tempest
David Greig	Theatre Workshop
John Guare	Judy Upton
Mark Haddon	Timberlake Wertenbaker
Peter Handke	Roy Williams
David Harrower	Snoo Wilson
Jonathan Harvey	Frances Ya-Chu Cowhig
Iain Heggie	Benjamin Zephaniah

Bloomsbury Methuen Drama Contemporary Dramatists
include

John Arden (two volumes)
Arden & D'Arcy
Peter Barnes (three volumes)
Sebastian Barry
Mike Bartlett
Dermot Bolger
Edward Bond (eight volumes)
Howard Brenton (two volumes)
Leo Butler
Richard Cameron
Jim Cartwright
Caryl Churchill (two volumes)
Complicite
Sarah Daniels (two volumes)
Nick Darke
David Edgar (three volumes)
David Eldridge (two volumes)
Ben Elton
Per Olov Enquist
Dario Fo (two volumes)
Michael Frayn (four volumes)
John Godber (four volumes)
Paul Godfrey
James Graham
David Greig
John Guare
Lee Hall (two volumes)
Katori Hall
Peter Handke
Jonathan Harvey (two volumes)
Iain Heggie
Israel Horovitz
Declan Hughes
Terry Johnson (three volumes)
Sarah Kane
Barrie Keeffe
Bernard-Marie Koltès (two volumes)
Franz Xaver Kroetz
Kwame Kwei-Armah
David Lan
Bryony Lavery
Deborah Levy
Doug Lucie

David Mamet (four volumes)
Patrick Marber
Martin McDonagh
Duncan McLean
David Mercer (two volumes)
Anthony Minghella (two volumes)
Tom Murphy (six volumes)
Phyllis Nagy
Anthony Neilson (two volumes)
Peter Nichol (two volumes)
Philip Osment
Gary Owen
Louise Page
Stewart Parker (two volumes)
Joe Penhall (two volumes)
Stephen Poliakoff (three volumes)
David Rabe (two volumes)
Mark Ravenhill (three volumes)
Christina Reid
Philip Ridley (two volumes)
Willy Russell
Eric-Emmanuel Schmitt
Ntozake Shange
Sam Shepard (two volumes)
Martin Sherman (two volumes)
Christopher Shinn
Joshua Sobel
Wole Soyinka (two volumes)
Simon Stephens (three volumes)
Shelagh Stephenson
David Storey (three volumes)
C. P. Taylor
Sue Townsend
Judy Upton
Michel Vinaver (two volumes)
Arnold Wesker (two volumes)
Peter Whelan
Michael Wilcox
Roy Williams (four volumes)
David Williamson
Snoo Wilson (two volumes)
David Wood (two volumes)
Victoria Wood

For a complete listing of Bloomsbury
Methuen Drama titles, visit:

www.bloomsbury.com/drama

Follow us on Twitter and keep up to date
with our news and publications

@MethuenDrama